D1314320

CONTROVERSY ADVERTISING

International Advertising Association

This study of how advertisers present points of view in
public affairs worldwide is the fourth in a series sponsored by the Sustaining and Organizational Members of
the International Advertising Association. It has been
prepared with the cooperation of IAA Chapters and the
collaboration of major advertisers, advertising agencies,
and media. The analytical text and case examples were
prepared by Albert Stridsberg, Associate Professor (Adj.)
of International Business at New York University, and
Editor of the quarterly publication, *Advertising World*.

Other publications
in the IAA series:

The Global Challenge to Advertising, New York: IAA,
1973.

*Effective Advertising Self-Regulation: a survey of current
world practice and analysis of international patterns*,
New York: IAA, 1974.

Progress in Effective Advertising Self-Regulation, New
York: IAA, 1976.

CONTROVERSY ADVERTISING

How Advertisers

Present Points of View

in Public Affairs

A Worldwide Study

Sponsored by
INTERNATIONAL ADVERTISING ASSOCIATION
Sustaining and Organizational Members

COMMUNICATION ARTS BOOKS

Hastings House, Publishers · New York 10016

Library of Congress Cataloging in Publication Data

International Advertising Association (Founded 1938)
    Controversy advertising.

    (Communication arts books)
    "The analytical text and case examples were
prepared by Albert Stridsberg."
        1. Advertising.   2. Advertising—Psychological
aspects.   3. Advertising, Public service.
I. Stridsberg, Albert B.   II. Title.
HF5828.I57   1977   659.1   76-56361
ISBN 0-8038-1214-0
ISBN 0-8038-1215-9 pbk.

IAA Sustaining Members

Axel Springer Verlag AG, Hamburg
Bacardi International Ltd., Hamilton, Bermuda
Banco de Intercambio Regional S.A., Buenos Aires
BBDO International, Inc., New York City
Dentsu Advertising Ltd., Tokyo
L. M. Ericsson, Stockholm
The Gillette Company, Boston
Gruner + Jahr AG & Co., Hamburg
International Telephone and Telegraph Corporation, New York City
International Business Machines Corporation, Armonk, New York
Leo Burnett Company, Inc., Chicago
L'Oréal, Paris
Marsteller International, New York City
Mauro Salles/Inter-Americana de Publicidade S.A., São Paulo
McCann-Erickson International, New York City
Nestlé Alimentana, Vevey, Switzerland
Newsweek Inc., New York City
N. V. Philips' Gloeilampenfabrieken, Eindhoven, Holland
Empresa Jornalistica Brasileira O Globo, Rio de Janeiro
Philip Morris Europe S.A., Lausanne

Reader's Digest Association, Pleasantville, New York
Régie No. 1, Paris
Rockwell International, Pittsburgh
Time Magazine, New York City
Uniroyal, Inc., New York City

IAA Organizational Members

Associação Brasileira de Anunciantes, São Paulo
European Association of Advertising Agencies, Brussels
Instituto Nacional de Publicidad, Madrid
Vereinigung der Werbeleiter und Werbeassistenten SRV, Zürich

Contents

CASE EXAMPLES

Foreword

HERE ARE THE underlying premises originally adopted for this study:

That the current use of advertising by corporations and governments to take positions on issues of public controversy represents a new kind of advertising technique, which responds to current needs for communication. That it is a worldwide trend, now being executed effectively and with great impact in a number of countries. That, because it is increasingly needed, it will continue to expand, both in volume within the countries where it is at present being used, and by extension to other countries where it has not yet been adopted. That, because of this increasing importance, the advertising industry of the world must take care to execute such advertising well and control it effectively.

The committee which recommended this project sought at first to avoid the somewhat alarming word "controversy." It was felt that, while the advertisers involved were certainly pursuing their own private interests, the subject matter of the various campaigns concerned "issues of public interest," and that, without exception, these advertisers believed that they were contributing to the public interest by expressing their opinions and working to mobilize or mold the opinions of other people through their advertisements. For this reason, the title originally proposed was "The Use of Advertising in the Public Interest."

In the initial explanation of the project to the Chapters of the International Advertising Association, this definition of the "use of advertising in the public interest" was offered:

Any kind of advertising that:

(a) Has been prepared professionally (by agency, consultant, or professional advertising staff).
(b) Appears in conventional advertising media, paid for by the advertiser sponsoring the campaign (not donated space or time).
(c) Is clearly indicated as advertising, and signed by the name of the firm or organization sponsoring the advertisements.
(d) Has as its principal subject matter some question of public interest, and not products or services.

We used, as examples of what we meant, the current campaigns of Mobil Oil Corporation and American Electric Power System (see Case Studies).

Methodology

Because of the multi-country nature of the project, we proposed to use the research method employed for a previous project (the IAA's *Effective Advertising Self-Regulation*, 1974), mailing "simple" questionnaires to 30 Chapters of the IAA in 24 countries. The questionnaires asked the Chapters to estimate the amount of advertising of this nature for the past three years and to identify trends, types of sponsoring organizations, types of media typically used, estimated amounts of expenditure by media, target audiences, and specific examples. Sample advertisements were requested, along with clippings of articles containing editorial comment.

At the time of mailing of the questionnaire, we were cautioned of the likelihood that what we called "advertising in the public interest" might be confused with "public service advertising." (See "Distinctions," beginning page 24.)

Initial response to the questionnaire in fact proved the merit of this caution. Only a few countries submitted reports about campaigns which qualified under our definition (U.S., U.K., Ireland, Germany, Turkey, Australia). Several sent us (or cited) advertising about controversial matters, but almost entirely of the public-service type.

Some responses showed reluctance to pursue the subject. Probing the countries which did not reply, we uncovered the view that this kind of advertising simply did not exist for all practical purposes.

At first, we assumed that confusion of our subject matter with the category of "public-service" was widespread. We learned, for example, that contrary to the practice in North America and France, public-service advertisements (encouraging blood donation, charity drives, energy conservation, etc.) are placed in many countries by the government, as *paid* advertising, and that this kind of government advertising expenditure is actually controversial in itself. Its magnitude in some countries was even alleged to have an influence on media fairness.

Checking back, we found that countries which had submitted public service advertising examples had, for the most part, not misunderstood our definition. Further probing revealed that, often, much of the business-government establishment was *opposed* to the use of advertising to play any kind of partisan role in matters of public controversy.

Re-evaluation

These findings did not sap the project of its value, but they did call into question most of the elements in the original proposition. Above all, they posed the question, *why?* If the assumptions in the original proposition were wrong, *why* were they wrong? We were forced to re-evaluate.

Reviewing the original proposition point by point, we had suggested, first, that

the current use of advertising . . . to take positions on issues of public controversy represents *a new kind of advertising technique* . . .

Historical review showed that, while the level of expenditure for this kind of advertising had sharply increased in some countries recently, the basic techniques of using advertising in controversies have been around since time immemorial. Furthermore, they had been employed with considerably greater subtlety than is often the case at present. The question became, why the sudden escalation in the amount?

We had suggested that "it is a *worldwide trend* . . ." A good many of the countries reporting indicated that they did not agree. Not only, in their eyes, was it not a worldwide trend, but some were not eager that it become one. The question became, why only in certain countries, not in others?

We had assumed, in terms of the initially reported successes, that

it will *continue to expand,* both in volume within the countries where it is at present being used, and by extension to other countries. . . .

Given countries that reported no significant penetration, and given indications of substantial resistance to the concept as well as the practice, we could no longer casually assume the continuing expansion. In fact, we had to look more carefully at the countries where the level of activity was high to see if, in fact, it had started to fall back.

The final element of the proposition remains true, if perhaps self-evident. Wherever advertising is in use by any of the participants in public controversy, it is crucial that it be executed well and controlled effectively—both in the public interest, and because misuse in this sector could jeopardize the progress of conventional advertising to promote the sale of goods and services.

1

The Subject

ADVOCATES OF public causes have long used advertising space and time to carry their messages to the public. Similarly, business firms have found themselves engaged in controversy (or have chosen to engage in controversy) and have used advertising as one means to express a point of view, make factual corrections, enlist support, and even urge some kind of action. The amount of advertising of this nature was, however, limited.

During the past ten years or so, expenditures for advertising which plays a role in controversial situations has been rising in a number of countries, notably the U.S. and Great Britain. Individual business firms and other corporate entities (trade and professional associations, state corporations, nationalized industries, and multinational trading groups such as OPEC) are vigorously, even aggressively, using signed advertising to tell the publics of these countries where they stand on questions of public concern.

It has been impossible to estimate the amount of money being spent on this kind of advertising. The category is not one conventionally analyzed. The problem is not simply the physical one of amassing and estimating the value of the advertisements. It is also one of classifying. For every advertisement which explicitly shows its partisanship, there are hundreds which, containing only factual statements, implicitly involve themselves in current controversy. Selection of facts can be a way of taking sides. Beyond this, advertising for a product or services connected with a controversial issue—petroleum, electricity, whisky, even the celluloid eyes of a toy doll—may directly or indirectly contain some kind of partisan statement or advocacy in an otherwise innocuous "selling" text. Sorting out such information, and giving it a weight in money value, is simply not possible.

Nonetheless, we know that the category is growing because the volume of all communications about controversies is growing, and the number of controversies engaging public attention appears to be growing. Further, the controversies themselves have spread across national frontiers.

Thus, the specific case examples discussed in the latter part of this volume will surprise no one, in whatever country. The issues are the ones basic to the second half of our century: the best means of producing, allocating, consuming and conserving energy; the respective roles of private enterprise and government in economic affairs; how best to combine economic productivity with long-term protection of natural resources and the environment in which we must live; freedom of the individual vs. the community interest; preservation of the traditional as opposed to the need for productive efficiency; and even, more recently, the rights of whole nations to a fair evaluation of their economic importance and needs.

In countries where advertising is accepted as a conventional part of public dialogue, it is perhaps inevitable that discussion of these issues in paid advertising should escalate as their significance becomes increasingly apparent.

Problems of terminology

Discussion of the subject is made difficult by the fact that there has been no agreed-upon term for this kind of advertising. A few of the expressions proposed have included:

public-interest advertising
public-affairs advertising
cause-and-issue advertising
public-issue advertising
viewpoint advertising
strategic advertising
opinion advertising
advocacy advertising
adversary advertising

The terminology in English is very unsatisfactory, and efforts in French (for example, "la publicité engagée," which has been rejected for "left-wing" connotations) and other languages have proved no better.

The variations on "public-interest," "public-affairs," and "public-issue" all evoke the expression "public-service." But "public-service advertising" is used specifically in the advertising industry of most countries to refer to the kind of advertising which is governmentally or para-governmentally sponsored and which promotes causes and activities which are widely accepted as desirable. "Public-service advertising" urges courses of action which are *not* controversial (except perhaps to a lunatic fringe).

"Viewpoint" and "opinion" advertising fail because they are vague and lack the urgency which is a component, however deeply buried, of any advertising on a controversial subject. Every advertisement contains an element of opinion—expresses a point of view—if only in the selection and presentation of the facts that it marshalls.

"Advocacy" and "adversary" advertising pose a different problem. Both suggest strident, aggressive expression of a point of view. Both carry connotations of litigation (as do their translations into other languages). Beyond this, John O'Toole, President of Foote, Cone & Belding and a recognized advocate of the use by business of advertising to express controversial opinions, has defined "advocacy advertising" in such a way as to limit it to the business establishment:

> . . . an advocate for the system and for individual corporations within that system. It is a different kind of advertising than most of us are used to, but it is a legitimate and, for the times, a highly appropriate mutation.
>
> ("Advocacy Advertising-Act II," a talk before the *Fortune Magazine* Corporate Communications Seminar, March 4, 1975)

O'Toole, like Herbert Schmertz of Mobil Oil, positions what he refers to as "adversary journalism" at the opposite political pole. In this way, the two words appear to have been steered into representing a political dichotomy: "advocacy" on the right and "adversary" on the left. Such political connotations, not inherent in the meanings of the words, discourage their use in our attempts at definition.

The word generally used to describe the use of communications to change, influence, or mobilize public opinion is *propaganda*. The expression "propaganda advertising" might be considered. However, at least in English, the word "propaganda" has strongly negative connotations.

The most acceptable expression available appears to be "controversy." This word implies a range of levels of activity from passive opposition to discussion and even dispute. It suggests a question at issue, but does not limit the number of points of view as would "dialogue." As it happens, the word translates, with almost precisely the same spelling, into most Western European languages.

Definition of the subject

We are now in a position to define what we are talking about in this book in such a way as to include all the different varieties of advertising that become involved, while making clear distinctions from other kinds of advertising (specifically certain kinds of product promotion, public-service advertising, and corporate-image communications) which are often confused with it.

> DEFINITION:
>
> *Controversy Advertising:* any kind of paid public communication or message, from an identified source and in a conventional medium of public advertising, which presents information or a point of view bearing on a publicly recognized controversial issue.

In essence, this definition separates controversy advertising from the general mass of advertising in terms of its *intention: to have bearing on a matter of recognized public controversy.*

The definition does not delimit the possible sources of such advertising. Obviously, it will mostly be generated by business firms and government, but the definition applies with equal validity to advertising underwritten by special-interest groups, religious groups, associations and clubs, political parties, and even individuals.

The definition does not focus upon a particular kind of result expected from the advertising. Correction of factual information, opinion change, mobilization of supporters, financial contributions, intervention through legislation, even riot and armed rebellion would qualify as objectives, without any category excluding any other.

The important elements of the definition should be emphasized. "Controversy advertising" is:

(1) *paid public communication*—As Hugh Holker of the Mirror Group Newspapers, London, points out, "this kind of advertising is the exact negation of public relations; it is clearly and identifiably paid for, not obtained on the basis of any kind of pretenses;"

(2) *with an identified source*—that is, a logotype or other kind of signature which indicates the true source of the information, opinion, or exhortation presented;

(3) *in a conventional medium of public advertising*—a context which clearly indicates the message to be advertised (rather than one so unconventional as to divert or mislead the audience so that they miss the point about its nature);

(4) *which presents information or a point of view*—any kind of message, in fact, which reflects an intent to participate in some way in the controversy at hand;

(5) *bearing on a matter of recognized public controversy*—recognition by the public exposed to the message that the issue being discussed is controversial.

The last point may seem overly academic. In fact, it is extremely relevant. As long as advertisements on certain subjects—for example, discouragement of drunkenness, promotion of safe driving, public discussion of venereal disease—are perceived as a reflection of generally agreed-upon social values, they are not controversial and are regarded as public-service advertising. The moment alternative possibilities are perceived, an issue becomes controversial.

Who uses this kind of advertising?

Historically and until quite recently, controversy advertising has normally been used by *some* types of participants, and not others, reflecting *some* controversial subjects, and not others.

Thus, social welfare organizations, even the most irresponsible, have traditionally run controversy advertisements, insofar as they could afford them. Anti-vivisection, labor union goals, extremist racial viewpoints—all have been the subjects of advertising tolerated in countries with strong advertising traditions.

Prior to the advent of television, a wide latitude was permitted for political advertising, by both individuals and parties, in countries with pluralistic governing systems and a tradition of open debate. (See the later section on "The problem of media access and suitability.")

On the other hand, questions of alternative economic systems were until recently relegated to the "balanced" presentation of textbook and classroom. With rare exceptions, questions of religious alternatives have not been expressed in advertising. But recent full-page advertisements for the Unification Church of the Rev. Sun Myung Moon, for the Church of Scientology, and for other newly-formed organizations raise new questions for the established churches about use of advertising in religious controversy.

Government organizations in many countries have regularly used donated advertising space and time to communicate social and economic policies that had been agreed upon through legislation or consensus, but only recently has the issue arisen of a government in power advertising a specific point of view *prior* to the resolution of a controversy. (For example, the U.S. Government campaign concerning energy policy; the British Government campaign concerning measures to curb inflation.)

In the business sector, economic and social positions have traditionally been advertised collectively, using as a voice the established industrial and professional associations. Individual corporations or business-men rarely addressed themselves to specific controversies in advertising. When they did, they were regarded as slightly peculiar by their peers, particularly if their points of view differed from the conventional industrial wisdom. Until recently, revolutionaries and adversaries of the "Establishment-culture" did not use advertising at all.

The range of advertisers using controversy advertising has been growing rapidly. Advertising is now the "first resort" of many a company or entity wishing to play an active role in a controversial situation, and even of those which, without intent to participate, nonetheless feel com-pelled to set the record straight (an important distinction).

Important points to note, however, are that:

(a) Certain industries tend to be much more outspoken than others. These include the petroleum, electric utility, and transportation in-dustries. Significantly, the level of controversy advertising is higher in these categories because *individual companies are using advertis-ing to express disagreement even among themselves concerning op-timum policy.*

(b) Other industries have remained silent while confronted with very major controversies, or have sought to express their positions through their industry associations. Notable examples in the U.S. are the Edison Electric Institute (until recently running advertisements on energy conservation without identifying Institute members by name) and the American Forest Institute (see Case Example).

Why is controversy advertising needed?

Very few people would propose to ban controversy advertising en-tirely, restricting advertising subject-matter solely to goods and services. At a time when Cesar Chavez's United Farm Workers use paid radio com-mercials and magazine advertisements to battle Gallo Wines and Califor-nia grape and lettuce growers, the "adversary culture" is obviously em-bracing advertising, not rejecting it.

Why does a company, or a private group, or a government unit, or even a counter-culture unit—that has heretofore kept silent or used non-paid routes to communications exposure—now turn to some kind of con-troversy advertising?

A combination of three determining elements seems to force such ad-vertising. These are the elements, expressed here in terms of corporate need:

1. *The corporation's constituencies will not tolerate silence.*

A reply to criticism, or even a position statement, is not demanded so much by the adversary as by the constituent. As Irving Kristol commented (in the *Wall Street Journal,* February 18, 1976):

> It is a traditional article of faith with corporations that the best strategy is one that does not give offense. Unfortunately, when you are in an adversary situation, the net effect of such a strategy is to persuade the public that, where one situation was able to generate so much smoke, there must also be fire.

Likewise, John Crichton, President of the American Association of Advertising Agencies, has written in a letter to Senator Philip A. Hart (July 16, 1974—quoted by Professor S. Prakash Sethi of the University of California, Berkeley, in his forthcoming volume, *Advocacy Advertising and Large Corporations: Social Conflict, Big Business Image, The News Media, and Public Policy*):

> Silence by a company in face of attacks upon its policies and practices is interpreted as an admission of guilt. Corporate advertising provides one avenue of self-defense.

Engulfed in what Barry Day, McCann-Erickson's Creative Director for Europe, has referred to as "a tidal wave of protestations of social and economic morality," the corporation is forced to make the best of a situation where it might prefer to remain silent.

On the other hand, Daniel Yankelovich, a leading examiner of U.S. public opinion and conscience, recently saw a bright side to the current disillusion and demand for candor. Speaking at the June, 1976, Conference on Business Credibility held in New York by the Conference Board, he commented:

> A decade ago, moral standards were so high, any disclosure was bound to lead to disillusionment. . . . Now people are so cynical, paranoid, and mistrustful that openness has to help, not hurt.

2. *The media are perceived by many companies to fail in their responsibilities; fair, accurate, or complete coverage in a controversy may not be obtained.*

Accusations of media failure, and fear of media environments, turn up in *every country studied* in the present survey. The counter-culture activist and his "establishment" brother are equally convinced of journalistic unfairness.

So far as reporting on business is concerned, Herbert Schmertz of Mobil Oil coined an expression for his reportorial attackers: "accusatory journalism." Irving Kristol comments on "journalistic media, about which everybody complains without doing anything. . . . That these media are biased against the business community is obvious." John O'Toole comments that "the voice of the adversary culture is more dominant in the media than that of the system. . . . (The media) deal in crisis and confrontation, the stuff of which news is made."

Various reasons for bias are given: the questioning role of the news media, which is considered traditional and necessary; the subsidizing of print media in many European countries by socialist governments or leftist political parties; other kinds of government control and/or coercion; above all, the outright independence of the professional journalist.

Whatever the cause of journalistic bias against business, leading advertising figures come to the same conclusion:

> *Neil O'Connor, Chairman of N. W. Ayer/ABH International:*
> Of necessity, in this climate, which seems to grow more partisan and hostile every day, business has had to look to paid advertising in order to present its side and make its points in public.
> *Gilbert Weil, attorney, before the Association of National Advertisers:*
> (Paid advertisements) allow the advertiser an opportunity to rehabilitate itself from any loss of good will which it might have suffered, or be threatened with suffering, as a result of these uncontrolled and independent activities by the news department of the broadcaster.
> *Harold Hoffman, Advertising Director of U.S. Steel:*
> Advertising provides us with the only way to economically reach large audiences with the story of our company when we want to without the 'benefit' of an editor, a writer, or a commentator. . . .

The media deny the failure of balanced coverage attributed to them. Like Gary Thorne, Display Advertising Director of the *Times* of London, they argue that the exigencies of covering the most important kinds of news make it impossible to allocate more than a certain amount of space to corporate information—and they admit that the role of news media is "to comment on the unusual rather than the usual." Peter Thomson, operating head of the U.K.'s Advertising Standards Authority, attributes the problem to the advertiser himself: "Media failure is not a lack of fairness in publishing both sides, but the advertiser wanting them to publish good news rather than bad."

3. *Advertisers taking part in public controversy want maximum control over the message delivered and the environment in which it is delivered.*

Whatever the truth may be, interviews with advertisers make it clear that the problem is not the *amount* of space or time involved, either in news about the advertiser and his colleagues, or about their adversaries, but the *way* in which such information is presented. Judicious phrasings get red-pencilled, subjected to unexpected juxtapositions with adversary material, or wrenchingly ad-libbed at the last moment.

The strength of advertising as a message carrier in controversy, according to Prakash Sethi, is that "the content of the message can be controlled and defined in a favorable manner," and the "environment of the message" can be similarly controlled, "thus making otherwise one-sided viewpoints appear objective and balanced."

2

Distinctions

ADVERTISING THAT IS intended to play a role in a public controversy sometimes may markedly resemble other kinds of advertising. As shall be discussed further on, there are some indications that the most effective controversy advertising is often that which is not conspicuously controversial.

The dividing line where conventional advertising ends and controversy advertising begins needs to be established specifically for three kinds of advertising: (1) "public-service" advertising, which promotes certain policies and courses of action for the general welfare; (2) product promotion, which under some circumstances is forced into advocacy of economic or social positions of controversy; and (3) "image" advertising, generally used to build a favorable reputation for the advertiser.

Controversy advertising and public-service advertising

Public-service advertising can be defined as communications presented in the conventional formats of advertising (i.e. typical newspaper or magazine space, radio or television time unit, in-town poster or country outdoor site, etc.) which urges its audience to implement or support some kind of social or economic action deemed beneficial by the consensus of the broad general public. Such advertising often carries a considerable amount of information, intended to educate the members of the audience unfamiliar with the reasons why the activity should be supported. Almost always, a public-service advertisement will specifically urge some kind of *action*.

Certain examples are found in almost every country, campaigns to

Support the Red Cross.
Donate blood to your local blood bank.
Prevent forest fires.
Prevent litter, because it pollutes the environment.
Save energy by avoiding unnecessary use.
Fasten your seat belt when driving or riding in an automobile.

In many countries it is easy to define such campaigns, since they are generally accepted and run by the major media at no cost. In the U.S., for example, a central organization created by all the major associations in the advertising field, The Advertising Council, accepts applications from groups wanting this kind of public-service advertising, recruits volunteer agencies to create and execute the campaigns on a non-profit basis, and arranges for the distribution of the materials to the major media. The media then use the materials as they see fit, on a wholly voluntary basis.

Similar systems function in other countries; for example, in France, Les Grandes Causes Nationales, and in Italy, Pubblicita e Propaganda.

In these countries, individual organizations and causes operating on a non-profit basis often prepare their own communications campaigns independently, and submit them to the media for diffusion at no cost. The burden is on the media, individually or through their associations, to determine if such independent campaigns are really "public-service" or not, and hence whether or not they qualify for free transmission.

Problems in connection with this system of voluntary preparation and use have recently provoked considerable discussion. Receiving no revenue for running the public-service messages, print media tend to use the smallest sizes offered, and to run the advertisements as "filler" to take up space at the last minute which has not been bought. Broadcast media, similarly, run such advertising in the un-sold time to be found in the "dead" periods of their daily schedules: the middle of the night, certain parts of the morning and afternoon when audiences are minimal. Only the public-service messages of exceptional creative interest receive better treatment: large space and good positions in print media, "prime time" on radio and television, and this as much for their entertainment/editorial value as for the nature of the cause being promoted.

Part of the problem in countries where public-service advertising is essentially voluntary, non-profit, and at no media cost, stems from the use of volunteer advertising agencies, arbitrarily assigned to the public-service projects. While out-of-pocket expenses may be reimbursed, the agency donates its most important asset—the time and talent of its people. When the agency is strongly motivated toward a public-service cause, or hopes to publicize its creative abilities by producing a campaign that will draw wisespread attention, the result may be remarkably effective. But campaigns have failed when the agency was reluctant to spend more than a minimum of its time and money. A lack-lustre job was done, and the media simply wouldn't use the advertisements offered them.

Dissatisfaction with the product of voluntary creative efforts has led to a definite trend in these countries to pay for the professional creation of public-service campaigns on a fee basis, with a profit factor built in. This is particularly true when the public-service campaign is directly sponsored by a government body. For example, the U.S. campaign against "drunk driving," where the Department of Transportation, working with the National Institute on Alcohol and Alcohol Abuse, has over a number of years commissioned Grey Advertising in New York City. The materials produced under such circumstances have been highly popular and have been given considerable exposure by the media.

No-cost media placement, and, to the lesser extent noted, volunteer preparation of the advertising at no cost are not essential to the definition of public-service advertising. In a number of countries, notably Scandinavia, public-service advertising campaigns are generally sponsored and coordinated by governmental or para-governmental organizations. These organizations generally pay advertising agencies to create and place the advertising, and the media, generally print, are paid normal rates for the space used. This means that the sponsoring organization has definite control over where and when the public-service messages will appear.

Outstanding examples of corporate sponsorship of public-service causes through paid advertising include: (1) the Esso "energy conservation" campaign run on German television during 1974 and 1975, described by many people as "a campaign the whole country loved;" (2) the Shell Oil Company "anti-litter" campaign run in the U.S. during the early 1970's, which strikingly dramatized the problem through four-color double-page spreads in magazines; and (3) the long-term campaign urging moderation in the consumption of alcoholic beverages, which has been running consistently in U.S. magazines since 1934, sponsored by Seagrams Distillers Company, one of the largest producers.

The dividing line between public-service communications and controversy advertising can be very fine, however. Examples:

"Fasten your seat belt every time you drive or ride." (A noncontroversial public-service message.) *"Fight for laws requiring seat belts on all cars."* (A distinctly controversial message some years back.)

"Control rats and vermin" is readily acceptable, especially when expressed as *"Starve a rat today."* (campaign in New York City,

created by Young & Rubicam for the Advertising Council in 1968). But *"Demand real estate regulations to reinforce voluntary efforts at rat and vermin control"* engaged the same basic cause in immediate controversy.

"Control population through the use of contraceptive pills and devices, and through abortion" is regarded as an acceptable public-service message, even one to be sponsored by government authorities, in a number of countries. (See Case Examples.) In the U.S., such a message is subject to instant attack by the "Right to Life" movement.

A striking illustration of national differences concerns the attitudes toward advertsing of condoms for contraception and the prevention of venereal disease. Groups in the U.S. have only recently succeeded in persuading consumer magazines to carry discreet advertising for condoms, and the battle to gain access to television and radio is still going on. In Sweden, by contrast, the campaign to encourage condom use is a public-service effort sponsored by the Government, employing print and TV visuals which, in other markets, would be considered in unacceptable taste.

What appears to be public-service advertising can easily slip over the line into controversy advertising. This occurs when:

(1) The social or economic action advocated is disputed by a significant sector of the population, possibly because of new information which conflicts with the "conventional wisdom."

(2) What is, *per se*, a neutral, positive kind of activity is viewed in terms of alternative possibilities and the "trade-offs" involved.

(3) The "conventional wisdom"—that is, what the "Establishment" assumes to be the consensus of its country or culture about "the right thing to do"—is confronted by the obstinate desire of a large segment of the public to do otherwise.

Here are examples to illustrate these points:

The long-popular "Smokey the Bear" campaign in the U.S., urging people to prevent forest fires, has abruptly met with resistance from environmental scientists who claim that forest fires are a vital part of reforestation. While this opposition does not destroy the value of the campaign, it has forced a shift in rationale from that of environmental conservation to one of public safety.

Two classic examples of the "trade-off" problem have recently involved major governments in controversy. In Great Britain, the Labor Government in 1974 proposed to use advertising messages to mobilize the business community, and the general public, to fight inflation. Resisting

Public-service campaign in Sweden (1973) to reduce venereal disease rate promoted use of controversial product
and employed visualizations which would be considered
highly controversial in many other countries. The campaign, which used newspaper advertising, poster, cinema, bumper stickers, and direct mail, was sponsored by
the Swedish League for Sexual Enlightenment, in cooperation with national health authorities, and created by
the Stockholm agency, Faltman & Malmen. An example
of how consensus decision-making can turn controversial
advocacy into public-service advertising.

(See pages 27, 68, and Case Examples.)

inflation is a natural "public-service" objective, the kind of thing everybody wants to support. However, the message was to be associated with
the specific policies advocated by the Government for control of inflation.
When finally produced, the campaign was unable to employ U.K. broadcast media for its first two phases. On the one hand, its themes could not
be submitted to the BBC as non-commercial public-service messages,

nor, on the other, were they appropriate for the commercial television and radio stations, since the regulations establishing these media would exclude the messages as *advocating policy* rather than simply promoting public welfare. (See Case Example.)

In the same way, the U.S. Advertising Council declined to undertake a campaign requested by the Federal Energy Administration concerning energy *policy* (although the Council had already coordinated a previous fuel conservation campaign, "Don't Be Fuelish"). The reason for the refusal was that the government proposed in its advertising message to list specific measures that the country should take—measures with which a number of sectors, including some petroleum and energy companies, were not in agreement.

In both cases, what was involved was not just opposition but the perception of "trade-offs." The British Government's policies to counter inflation may or may not have been the right ones. No one would dispute the value of resisting inflation, but acceptance of *policy* involved trading-off certain values against others—inflation control against economic growth, for example. Likewise, the U.S. government's desire to establish an optimum energy policy could only be praised. But when specific measures were proposed, a number of private sectors quickly perceived that they involved sacrificing or curtailing other economic and social values.

The most surprising cases where public-service messages abruptly become controversy advertising, or, as Barry Day of McCann-Erickson Europe calls them, "special pleading," involve unexpected public resistance. In these cases, a campaign embarked upon for what would appear obvious social or economic benefits is suddenly greeted with antagonism, to the point of counter-campaigns being spontaneously organized.

Good examples are the German Government effort to obtain acceptance of speed limits on the autobahns in 1974, and the U.S. Government effort to promote the U.S. 1976 Bicentennial.

The German authorities, using outdoor posters along the autobahns to promote the speed limits, were answered by a campaign of bumperstickers, organized and supported by the ADAC. This enormous club for automobile owners also reportedly allocated advertising space for its campaign in the club's important consumer magazines. The campaign, featuring the slogan "Frei bürger fordern freie fahrt" (Free citizens demand free driving, or driving freedom), swept Germany like wildfire. It is apparently a matter of embarrassment in retrospect, given the semi-governmental role which the ADAC plays.

In the same way, the U.S. Government set out to promote the country's 200th anniversary with a wide range of activities, many involving the use of advertising and sales promotion. Quite unexpectedly, the Bicentennial activities were opposed by an organization calling itself The People's Bicentennial Commission, which challenged many of the values and assumptions underlying the Bicentennial activities. Using sophisticated market research and an "adversary" advertising agency, the People's Commission opposed particularly strongly a "public-service" project of the U.S. Advertising Council: an effort to improve awareness and understanding of the American economic system. The emergence of this "adversary" group underlines the fact that the Advertising Council's campaign is not one of public-service, but an example of controversy advertising.

In the new atmosphere of challenge, the restrained efforts of organizations like the Advertising Council to uphold public values without engaging in controversy seem increasingly difficult. Subjects which used to be handled as public service advertising are now being treated as potentially controversial, exposed to the danger of negative public reaction. This imposes new requirements of professionalism in creative approach, attitudinal research, and media targeting. To obtain the needed quality, countries where public-service advertising has been produced at no cost are finding it necessary to pay at commercial rates for what they get.

Two examples of this, drawn from the U.S., are (1) the series of paid advertisements in the style of articles, in the U.S. editions of the *Reader's Digest*, presented to considerable effect by an organization of business firms, The Business Roundtable, to explain the workings of the U.S. free-market system; (2) the use of paid radio and television advertising by the municipal police force in Dallas, Texas, to fight crime by building public awareness of safety precautions. Both campaigns, professionally prepared, hover on the border between public service and controversy.

Where product promotion ends and "product advocacy" begins.

A second sector where a distinction must be drawn is between advertising for the promotion of goods and services *per se*, which is the basis of the advertising industry as we know it, and advertising in which the nature of the product or service being promoted involves the advertisers in controversy. In this situation, the use of the product (or service) is disputed by one or more adversary groups for larger economic and social reasons than simply that of product efficiency.

There have always been products under this kind of attack, notably tobacco products, alcoholic beverages, cosmetics, toys, and proprietary drugs, chiefly because of their alleged harm to individuals using them. More recently, the attacks have extended to a much wider range of products and services, and the grounds for attack have extended to a greater number of societal concerns. Some examples:

Packaging materials. Products have frequently been launched in new packaging intended to improve convenience. Packaging materials have been strongly criticized by consumer and environmentalist groups. These attacks are directed at the consequences, real or alleged, of the sale and use of whole classifications of packaging. Thus, certain types of disposable plastic bottles and boxes have been attacked because they do not deteriorate, but persist and "damage the environment" if special measures are not taken to destroy them. Another allegation concerns the use of fluorocarbons as propellants in aerosol "squirt" or "spray" packaging. It is charged that the chemical, persisting in the upper atmosphere, may dissipate the ozone layer which protects life against harmful radiation from the sun. (See du Pont Case Example.)

Ingredients. Various ingredients in consumer products— colorants, flavors, stabilizers, sweeteners, enhancers—have been alleged to endanger health.

Nutritional patterns. Many food products, innocuous in themselves, have been attacked on the grounds that people substitute them for other, more nutritious products. These attacks range from criticisms of "junk food" allegedly without nutritive content, through produce with high-sugar content which are thought to damage teeth and furnish only "empty calories," to products suspected of causing serious nutritional damage when incorrectly used (specifically, powdered milk and dry baby formula products as substitutes for breast feeding).

Product safety. This question has escalated from consideration of the individual product (*e.g.* the early attacks by Ralph Nader against the Corvair automobile) to whole classes of products. Thus, the issue has become, not the safety of the individual driver and his passengers, but the desirability of man's traveling on the earth's surface above certain speeds and, further, criticism of the internal combustion engine as inherently wasteful of energy and destructive of the environmental conditions favoring human life and health.

Increasingly, critics tend to attack the advertising of the offending products, rather than the products themselves. They reason that, if they can effectively interfere with a product's promotion, and hence its sales, they can more rapidly force the product's withdrawal. Continued advertising, without acknowledging such attacks, is taken as an admission of guilt or a deliberate effort to dismiss the charges by ignoring them. Advertising to clarify factual points is interpreted as hostile retaliation.

On the other hand, termination of the advertising under attack, or removal of the product or brand from the market, is automatically taken as a victory and so publicized—even when the action is a result of supply conditions or preparation to launch an improved version. (An example of this kind of misinterpretation of motive is the reaction to Mobil Oil Corporation's decision to withdraw from promotion of its U.S. gasoline brands in mid-1973. The action was taken a half-year before the OPEC-created petroleum crisis, as a voluntary effort on the corporation's part to avoid promoting consumption of a scarce resource. Oil industry critics persistently maintain that the decision was taken post-OPEC, and grudgingly, by a company beleaguered by the accusation of profiteering.)

It would seem that there is almost no way to terminate such a controversy, if the adversary side has the energy to keep it alive.

The difference between "corporate image" and corporate advocacy

A final much-needed clarification concerns the difference between advertising used to build a positive "corporate image" in the minds of one or more "publics," and use of advertising by a corporation to take an active role in a controversy.

Certain modes of controversy advertising may strongly resemble the conventional idea of "image advertising," and "image" campaigns may be bent to serve the persuasive goals of corporate engagement in controversy. Nonetheless, the objectives of the two kinds of advertising are markedly different, resulting in considerable differences in audiences chosen, creative and media strategies employed, and advertising content.

It should be noted that, in the course of our research, the majority of advertising agencies and media interviewed did not recognize this distinction between building of a company "image" in the public mind and direct or implicit advocacy of company positions and policies.

What is corporate image advertising? It is a kind of communication which, by the use of signed, paid messages by a company in conventional advertising media, seeks to obtain a desired level of public awareness and a maximum favorable impression among selected audiences. To do so, this kind of advertising communicates a carefully chosen range of facts to create an understanding of the company's activities, moral standards, policies, management style, and expectations.

In essence, corporate image advertising treats the company as if it were a product, positioning it with care within its industry or industries, giving it a clear differentiation from others resembling it, and basically "selling" it to the audiences selected. The selling objectives are usually financial, legal, and to a lesser extent governmental support, to facilitate the company's pursuit of its business objectives.

The origin of most image campaigns, in whatever the country, is the discovery not that people think badly of the company, but that they know little or nothing about it. In the past, and still today in many countries, a good many companies have liked it that way. The so-called "low profile," with minimum public awareness, is often considered the best means of avoiding interference in corporate affairs by external forces.

The "high profile" strategy, involving the construction and communication of a corporate image, has been the product of the stage in each country at which large corporations have faced the alternatives of either continuing to grow or falling behind the competition. These companies, often privately-held, perceived the need for outside financial resources in order to undertake the expansion required. To succeed in the quest for capital, increased visibility for the company of a favorable nature would be helpful. Building of a favorable image was considered particularly useful if a policy of diversification into a conglomerate structure had been chosen as the way to growth.

Corporate image planning, and the advertising which results from it, have been seen by critics as mostly cosmetic in nature. While this may not be entirely fair, it is true that corporate image communications are intended to tell what the company wants thought about it, nothing more nor less. The image is *designed,* and may reflect more what the company aspires to be than what it actually is. The communications may significantly omit information which does not contribute to the effect desired. Like product advertising, corporate image communications seek to make little-known companies better known, and to extend known favorable aspects to lesser-known corporate units.

Corporate image advertising does *not* concern itself with problems unless there are solutions to be proferred, and plausible ones. Such communication asks no action on the part of its audiences beyond the passive approval and favorable attitude conducive to making financial agreements and obtaining government approvals. It does not confront antagonists with a point of view, nor does it demand from its audiences an examination of conscience, or commitments, or partisan activity.

As will be seen in the next section, corporations use advertising in a markedly different manner in situations of controversy. First, the company and its counselors are not free to choose the information they employ in such advertising. Information selection is determined by the nature of the controversy, which exists *outside* the company. Little or no effort is made to differentiate the advertiser from other companies holding the same viewpoint.

Second, the purpose of controversy advertising is not to create a passively favorable climate for actions the company wants to take, but to inject the company's interests, points of view, and objectives into the outside controversy where other people are taking actions.

Third, whether the company's position is defensive or aggressive, its use of advertising *per se* involves taking a kind of action, not just creating a preparatory atmosphere. Even the kind of controversy advertising which most resembles the image approach (see the section on "The platform of fact") involves an action to define the company position and establish its right to a voice in a particular controversy. It is this last point—the specific focus of controversy advertising—which is possibly the most significant point of difference between controversy advertising and corporate image communications.

The difference between the two is also reflected in results. The results of corporate image work are measured in terms of public opinion. The results of controversy advertising are measured in terms of practical action and historical event. Negative results for corporate image advertising involve, at worst, public disbelief and money wasted. When controversy advertising goes wrong, the negative impact may turn up in falling stock prices and sales, and in regulatory or legislative action, labor turbulence, and social agitation.

3

Three Postures of Advertising in Controversy

AMONG THE MANY mis-impressions about corporate use of advertising in public controversy, one is particularly prevalent. This is the assumption that, because a company's decision to employ advertising under circumstances of controversy is a *reaction* to the situation, the content and posture of the advertising will necessarily be *defensive*.

A parallel assumption is that, when adversary organizations attack individual corporations or the so-called "Establishment," their advertising and other communications are essentially aggressive.

In fact, the IAA survey of countries where controversy advertising is in considerable use suggests the contrary. The characteristic business approach reflects little urgency to defend actions and policies, but a rather strong motivation to resolve conflict in a positive manner, by offering solutions. On the other hand, the characteristic adversary posture—protest— is a defensive one. It is the protesters who feel victimized or consider that they are acting on behalf of victims.

Further, it is not always the case that a controversial issue pits a business firm against a public group. In many current controversies involving the use of advertising, different sectors of the business community are debating each other in a "battle of the advertisements."

In addition to defense and aggression, there is a third posture in controversy advertising, particularly as it is used by business: exercising the *right* to participate in a given controversy.

These then are three postures in controversy advertising which emerge from analysis of the case examples from a dozen or more countries:

1. Defense of an economic or social point of view.
2. Aggressive promotion of a point of view.
3. Establishment of a "platform of fact" which entitles the advertiser to have a voice in the controversy, and to participate in its resolution.

Defense

At the outset, a distinction must be made between controversy advertisements using a defensive posture and advertising undertaken, *not* to engage in controversy but simply to correct or clarify matters of fact. Corporations which have no intention of participating in public debate may find themselves constrained by mis-representation to employ advertising for this purpose. To do so is a clear obligation of management to the owners or stockholders, and to the employees as well. Correction of fact is intended to eliminate, rather than indulge in, controversy. The amount of fact-correcting advertising, as revealed in our survey, is relatively low, since factual misrepresentation is usually corrected by media in their dedication to publish the truth.

Defensive use of controversy advertising appears, from the evidence gathered, to take two forms:

(a) the effort to retaliate by justifying or explaining situations in which the advertiser concedes there were alternative courses of action, and
(b) portrayal of the attacked party—whether corporation, professional association, or public group—as "victim."

The first category implicitly suggests that the opposing point of view not only has wide acceptance, but has eroded the loyalty of the advertiser's natural constituency: stockholders, management and technical cadres, union members, customers. Presentation of the rationale for past actions is required.

The IAA multinational survey indicated that the few examples of this kind of defensive advertising were found mostly in the U.S. and Great Britain. The advertisement in the Mobil series, "What about those obscene profits?", could be construed as a defensive explanation. In the same way, certain of the advertisements in the Tate & Lyle series from Great Britain have sought not only to present the facts concerning the company's market position, but also a defensive case explaining why the position is not the negative one alleged. Both examples occur, however, in the course of continuing campaigns in which other advertisements propose a range of positive, non-defensive goals!

In a similar manner, a number of major controversy campaigns have their point of departure in defensive need, but have moved on almost immediately into explanation of positive aspects. Examples include the du Pont (U.S.) campaign concerning aerosol fluorocarbons, the Hamburger Electrizitätswerke campaign on nuclear generation of energy, and the ITT campaigns in Europe concerning the corporation's contributions to the various national economies.

The second category of defense—portraying the advertiser as victim of unjustified attacks—is a difficult posture for business corporations and other groups, although some companies have succeeded in so positioning themselves.

For example, when several U.S. automobile companies contemplated launching an advertising campaign in the mid-1960's to counter Congressional hearings into automotive safety, using as their argument that ill-calculated regulation could damage a significant sector of the American economy, they were reluctantly advised by several large advertising agencies that this position would not be believed and might backfire, doing more harm than good.

However, when the opposition is not drawn from consumer or special interest groups, but rather large corporate competitors, Government units, or legislative bodies, corporations do not hesitate to cast themselves in the victim's role. A number of the advertisements in the American Electric Power series (see U.S. Case Examples) which portray AEP as battling Big Government, in this case the Environmental Protection Administration, carry conviction. In a similar way, the Bristol Channel Ship Repairers' campaign to fight the British government's efforts to nationalize the firm, with Anthony Wedgwood Benn personifying a faceless bureaucracy, was reported to be immediately credible, not simply to a management audience, but also on the shop-floor level. (See U.K. Case Examples.)

Active advocacy of an economic or social point of view

"The best defense is a strong offense" is a well-worn cliché, but one which comes to mind in connection with corporate use of advertising in controversy. The advertiser literally *protests* against the opposing point of view, and in so doing offers more or less specific alternatives of his own.

The most talked-about examples of controversy advertising—really qualifying for the expression "advocacy"—fall into this category: the Chesapeake & Ohio campaign in 1945 demanding a modification of railroad policy; the counter-culture's advertisements opposing California grape and lettuce growers, Gallo wine, and slumlords; the Dutch music lovers' volunteer efforts to save the pirate radio ship *Veronica;* the Chase

Manhattan Bank advertisements giving precise recommendations about "capital shortfall."

Surprisingly, while these types of advertisements proposing specific action are the most conspicuous, they are not the most numerous. This approach, while "confronting" the opposition, sometimes runs the risk of antagonizing the advertiser's own constituents as well. Further, corporations are prudent about making recommendations which are so specific as to lose validity and require modification as circumstances change.

Establishment of a "platform of fact"

Sophisticated companies are increasingly devoting their communications funds to advertising which presents the factual relationship between their activities and issues of public concern and controversy. Such advertisers include companies, like Philips of Eindhoven, which have not been subjected to attack but wish their involvement in societal issues made known. In the event that such a corporation wants later on to make an active policy recommendation, its right to a voice will already be recognized by significant segments of the public.

This kind of advertising, as noted earlier, bears a strong resemblance to corporate image advertising. The advertisements are factual, do not present demands for action of justification of past events, and represent a selection of information intended to put the corporation in a good light.

The intent in these cases, however, is not to create a favorable climate for financial activity and corporate development, but to create a "platform of fact" in the public mind, to which reference can be made should the corporation find it advisable to use advertising to communicate to the public at some future date its position in a controversy. John O'Toole of Foote Cone & Belding took note of this kind of advertising in his talk to the 1975 *Fortune Magazine* conference on corporate communications:

> The dialogue with the public should begin long before the company or industry is under siege. . . The acceptance and credibility built up through this kind of long-range program is beyond price should you have to suddenly present that reader with your viewpoint on a highly controversial issue.

He refers further to companies which "work, over time, to project . . . a communications identity from which issue-oriented messages can be presented as needed. . . . (Such messages are) more apt to be accepted when they come from someone known and liked." The content of such advertising is not designed to build corporate image. It does not attempt to portray the whole corporation, but to explain its involvement in specific issues. The strategy further differs from the image approach in terms of audiences addressed (see later section on "Public means publics.")

But the basic objective is precise—to implant in the minds of the audiences likely to be concerned a predisposition to listen, when or if the corporation chooses to voice its opinion on a specific subject.

Campaigns of this nature are multiplying rapidly in Europe, the Far East, and North America. They are increasingly popular because (a) they provide opportunities for highly sophisticated creative approaches, framed in the context of long-term objectives; (b) they do not pose the problems of media access which both the defensive and active controversy-advertising categories may encounter; and (c) they do not invite casual retaliatory attack from adversaries.

Of the many available examples, an almost perfect prototype of the use of "platform advertising" is the current corporate campaign in the U.S. by Union Carbide. In the campaign a continuing series of advertisements about Carbide activities (inconspicuously oriented toward areas of controversy) is targeted at the many audiences on whose support Carbide depends. Having gained this support, Carbide can confidently employ periodic advocacy advertisements targeted precisely at a much narrower audience of legislators, government officials, and top decision-makers. (See U.S. Case Examples.)

4

Origins and Development
of Controversy Advertising

It is recognized that the use of advertising in public controversy sharply increased in a number of countries beginning approximately in mid-1973. By far the greatest growth apears to have been in the U.S., with appreciable growth also in Great Britain, Germany, and Japan. This statement is an overall conclusion from our survey, although it has been impossible to identify with any precision the amounts of expenditure in any of the countries.

The increase has been both quantitative and qualitative:

1. Corporations, associations, and public interest groups turned to explicit advertising campaigns to advocate their points of view.
2. Responding to controversies affecting their products and operations, many corporations injected a note of opinion or introduced relevant factual content into their existing programs of corporate and productf advertising.
3. In a number of countries, government-sponsored public-service advertising campaigns shifted toward direct or indirect advocacy of controversial policies.

The use of advertising to support one side or another in public controversies was by no means news. The question is: Why did it suddenly blossom in 1973, and what has caused it to take its present forms?

Earlier examples of the role of advertising in controversy

Scholars have only just begun to research the subject. Tracing early examples of controversy advertising is made difficult by the fact that it has never been considered as a separate category and labeled as such. Most of it has disappeared into a vast, undifferentiated category referred to today as "corporate advertising," but for many years awkwardly labeled "institutional advertising," leading to confusion with advertising for hospitals, orphanages, and educational facilities.

It is possible to sketch, in a cursory way, some of the background. The possibility of using advertising to play a role in controversy has existed as long as advertising has been recognized as a specialty. Politicians in democratic societies during the 18th and 19th centuries regularly had recourse to handbills and newspaper advertisements to put forward their points of view. If companies did not use such methods at the time, it was apparently because (1) they did not use much advertising at all, and (2) they did not want their company names to appear alongside much of the irresponsible material being published. Probably most important, media had not yet emerged that could reach the audiences the companies might have wanted to address, at least in any economical way.

During the First World War, advertising was used by all sides as a method of evoking patriotic fervor, and public-service messages were used for various war-effort purposes. At that time, advertising media and printing technology were both developing rapidly, and the first agencies using the "full-service" concept were being organized. Not by chance, the advertisement, "The Penalty of Leadership," for Cadillac Motor Company was written by a pioneer advertising agency man, Theodore F. Mac-Manus. This advertisement, chosen by Julian Watkins in 1948 as one of the "100 Greatest Advertisements" of U.S. advertising history, advocated maintaining standards of quality, even at the expense of competitive position. Generally taken as a classic statement of operating philosophy, the advertisement was in fact conceived as a defense of a faulty product (the original "51" Model Cadillac, which broke down frequently because of faulty wiring) and then transformed into aggressive advocacy of a corporate point of view.

Preliminary research has produced no notable examples of the use of advertising in controversy in the U.S. during the 1920's, with the exception of a campaign to promote advertising itself, featuring a spokesman named "Andy Consumer." In Europe, the techniques of advertising—particularly urban posters—were taken over by radical movements, and the long tradition of social-consciousness outdoor advertising, frequently executed by artists of stature, was begun.

During the 1930's, use of advertising to express the points of view of labor unions and associations of small businessmen became significant in the U.S. Organizations like the International Ladies Garment Workers Union (ILGWU) showed surprising ingenuity, at one point producing a stage review, "Pins and Needles," which toured the country to promote the cause of the union and the purchase of U.S. goods against cheaper foreign competition. (The campaign continues to this day in television and radio commercials using a "musical show" format, with transcription of the musical jingle published as a supporting advertisement in magazines.)

Business use of advertising to express points of view was still regarded in the U.S. as slightly eccentric during the 1930's. The long-term chairman of the International Latex Company ("Playtex" products) began a series of discursive editorial advertisements toward the end of the decade, presenting his signed personal point of view—for many years paid for by the company. The Warner & Swasey series (see Case Example), presenting a conservative point of view about the values of private enterprise, began to appear in U.S. business magazines in 1936.

In England, about this time, a significant step toward controversy advertising was taken when publicly held corporations (limited companies) developed the practice of advertising, in addition to the required balance sheets and financial statements, a "statement of the Chairman's remarks" to the annual meeting. Ostensibly published for the information of stockholders and members of the investment community unable to attend, the advertisements explicitly communicated policies which those companies advocated for their own and for general public interest. To this day, such advertisements remain a major element in British corporate advocacy. While never adopted as a general practice in the U.S., and little used elsewhere, they have furnished a strong public example of a policy of corporate disclosure and open declaration of objectives.

In many countries during the 1930's, aspiring artists and writers were constrained, by economic circumstances, to take jobs in business. Many went to work in advertising agencies and company advertising departments, in spite of uncongenial economic and political opinions. A tradition of expert knowledge, particularly of graphics, was founded at that time which would become important in the counterculture movements following the Second World War.

During World War II, all nations used their communications industries in their war efforts. In the battle of words, many executives and specialists from advertising and marketing gained experience in the use of propaganda, both the "black" kind involving distribution of un-truth from concealed or misidentified sources, and the "white" kind, which was the equivalent of signed, paid controversy advertising. Considerable experience in communicating government policy was accumulated. Such communications, however politically motivated, were accepted as public information and in the public service thanks to the phenomenon of public consensus generated during that time of war.

Following the war there was preoccupation in Western Europe and the Far East with rebuilding society and industry, and in the U.S. with maintaining national security, digesting an extraordinary expansion of communications with the arrival of television, and coping with an equally remarkable expansion of the total economy.

Indications of the new use of advertising in controversy began to appear. In 1951, Britain, still under conditions of austerity, was exposed to a noteworthy campaign using cartoon drawings and sponsored by an industrial group to favor private enterprise. The campaign theme, "Free Enterprise Gives Everyone a Chance," was highly controversial at the time, and the advertising came to an end when the Labor Government took office. At the same time, the Tate & Lyle Campaign (see Case Example), while confined to messages on packaging, set a classic pattern for future campaigns of this nature.

The election of President John F. Kennedy in 1960 roughly coincided with the turnaround in the economies of Western Europe. The charismatic personality of the young President, combined with substantial media skills employed on his behalf, rapidly produced favorable worldwide reaction from the emerging "youth generation." Strong attitudes of social awareness, with optimism about the possibility of accomplishing new goals, were built up.

About this time, in many countries—not just the U.S. and Great Britain, but most Western European countries, Japan, and industrialized countries like Argentina, Brazil, and South Africa—educational opportunities were extended downward into the mass of the population. Young people who, in previous generations, would have left school and started as manual laborers were exposed to higher levels of education. Significant for the advertising industry was the creation of a new talent pool of semi-trained commercial artists, copywriters, and television producers drawn from blue-collar environments.

The history of their drift into contributing their skills to political advertising, and thereafter to volunteer campaigns in support of social and economic causes, has yet to be written. If, during the period, any single event can be described as the watershed—the point at which these people, and the general advertising community worldwide, became aware of the new possibilities for using advertising in controversy—it was in September, 1964, during the U.S. presidential campaign. The supporters of Lyndon Johnson broadcast a one-time TV spot showing a child, a dandelion, and an atomic explosion, with the message, "Elect Lyndon Johnson."

This single political advertisement, prepared by the Johnson campaign's advertising agency, Doyle Dane Bernbach, was as much a bombshell to the advertising business as it was to the electorate. It was commented upon worldwide, and it is still controversial today. (See the sections on "Problems for the future" and "The future?")

The impact of this single advertisement and its repercussions were to make the new generation of creative young advertising men aware of their power to affect the fortunes of social and economic causes. At a time when salaries for skilled creative people escalated rapidly in all major industrial countries, they found themselves in a position to donate their talents as volunteers. The "creative boutique" emerged, formed by teams of these restless young people who were willing to handle "cause" campaigns inexpensively as a means of demonstrating their abilities to persuade.

The contribution of the adversary culture

As far as IAA research has been able to trace, the abrupt escalation in the quantity and quality of controversy advertising began not as an effort on the part of corporate business, but as an almost inevitable product of a young generation of talented, experimental advertising people with strong political commitments.

Despite their youth, these workers were professionals, often employed by very large agencies or associated with the dominant schools for art and television training. In a major agency like Young & Rubicam International, New York, for example, public-service campaigns organized by the Advertising Council (such as the Urban Coalition's slum campaign, "Give a Damn," or the Peace Corps advertising) took on an aggressive tone with a distinctly controversial edge.

A top creative team at Doyle Dane Bernbach, Bert Steinhauser and Chuck Kolluwe, used their own time to create a print advertisement in support of the Rat Extermination Bill, "Cut this out and put it in bed next to your child." It drew nationwide attention and ensured the passage of legislation already defeated on the first vote. A smaller New York agency, Geer, Dubois, followed with a campaign for New York City's Health Department, "Starve a Rat Today," chosen by *Advertising Age* as one of the top ten campaigns in the U.S. in 1968. (See Case Examples.)

While these and similar campaigns were initially thought of as public-service, they fit the definition of controversy advertising, since they often conflicted with the interests and declared policies of real-estate organizations and other special-interest groups.

The inter-penetration between creative people in advertising and activists dabbling in the counter-culture was not so apparent in other countries during the late 1960's, but it was certainly present. Paul Siebel, Joint Managing Director of J. Walter Thompson Company in Germany, tells of having to force the departure of Daniel Bendit-Cohn, the French radical leader, from the agency's Frankfurt premises, where he had managed to find employment in the art studio.

Response to global events

These first excursions into controversy advertising were frequently small-scale and local or regional, and perceived at the time as public-service. The tone was one of bright optimism, which corresponded to the increasing fortunes and good fortunes of the young advertsing people involved, and the happy tenor of the so-called counter-culture.

A number of developments, on a global scale, caused a shift to bitterness, hostility, and the emergence of clearly-defined adversary efforts which employed advertising techniques against the declared policies of "the Establishment." These developments included: publication of the Club of Rome Report, raising major questions about population, environment, nutrition and energy; conflict between students and authorities in the U.S., France, Germany, Japan, Mexico, and elsewhere; the continued escalation of the Vietnam war.

Many of the "concerned youth" became adversary to the Establishment. They had not forgotten the effectiveness of advertising as a technique to get their way. Some moved out of the advertising agencies and companies where they had worked in order to form specialized units to produce "public-interest" advertising. Others joined forces wth various groups and movements as staff members specializing in advertising communications. It is possible to take note here of only a few of the adversary advertising activities which antedated the abrupt entry of major corporations into controversy advertising.

In mid-1969, a volunteer group of New York advertising people led by a Yale undergraduate, Ira Nerkin, and by David McCall, Chairman of the McCaffrey & McCall advertising agency, assembled a campaign to "Un-sell the War" in Vietnam. The campaign centered around a poster design, "I Want Out," showing a bandaged Uncle Sam begging to get out of the war. The poster gently parodied a famous U.S Army recruiting poster from World War I, showing Uncle Sam pointing his finger and saying, "I Want You!" (See Case Examples.)

The renowned copywriter, Howard Gossage, creator of the famous "Irish whiskey" campaign, became the central figure in a school of young advertising men on the U.S. West Coast, working as a consultant to the counter-culture's slick magazine, *Ramparts.* His San Francisco advertising agency, Freeman, Mander & Gossage, created in 1966 the first major environmental campaign for the Sierra Club, opposing dams on the Colorado River which would have inundated much of the Grand Canyon. Subsequent Gossage efforts fought for the preservation of the redwood forests in California, for national parks and monuments in several states, and against the development of the supersonic transport (SST).

Following Gossage's death in 1969, some of his young colleagues formed organizations such as Public Interest Communications, the Public Media Center and, in the East, the Public Advertising Council, In the Public Interest (a radio-television production group), Projects for Peace and The People's Bicentennial Commission. These groups have produced advertising of professional quality in opposition to legislation detrimental to the environment, high electric rates, nuclear generation of electric power, Gallo Wine labor practices, and, most recently, against the Advertising Council campaign to explain the U.S. economic system.

The corporations join in

Another turning point for U.S.-originated controversy advertising was reached just before the outbreak of Israeli-Arab hostilities in 1973. Mobil Oil Corporation, after study of the worldwide energy situation, terminated its campaigns of consumer gasoline promotion and shifted to a complex pattern of editorial-style advertisements and sponsorship of public broadcast programing which, slightly modified, continues today. (The Mobil campaign is discussed in detail in the section on Case Examples.) *Media Decisions* magazine has described mid-1973 as the "turning point for the oils toward advocacy advertising and a heightened trend among industries . . . (toward) a new spirit of social accountability. It was decided to explain policies and actions to the people via paid media. They started telling what was being done with the plants producing the goods, and why. . . . . They became more articulate about environmental problems. . . . (The corporation) found it had to communicate more openly not only with its customers, but also with government regulators, investors, and workers."

This change of direction occurred simultaneously with the eruption of hostilities in the Middle East and the subsequent oil embargo, and the onset of a severe recession in the U.S., which had actually been triggered before the petroleum crisis. Also, the return of the "youth generation," older and more subdued, to the Establishment seems to have coincided with an opportunity to employ their creative approaches in the service of business advocacy. To the extent that such advertising today is fresh and professional, it appears to stem from this particular generation, tested in the fires and passions of the 1960's.

If this very tentative review of advertising history has a thesis, then, it is that the sudden increase in controversy advertising within the past ten years resulted from a combination of the following:

Penetration of education and communications training downward into a much broader level of the postwar generation, creating a large pool of talent.

A sustained period of economic expansion, which encouraged independence, development of adversary opinion, and strong social motivations among youth.

Emergence of a series of controversial questions (environment, energy, population increase) upon which the new generation of advertising people focused their attention and sharpened their skills.

A subsequent shift in political and economic fortunes, motivating young advertising people to place their skills at the disposition of the Establishment, at the moment that corporate society perceived a significant need to use commercial advertising for expression of its policies.

It has been impossible to trace, in this initial survey, to what extent the U.S. sequence of events has occurred in other countries. Part of the uncertainty is ill-defined comparisons in salary levels in the advertising industry and the resulting degrees of independence of young advertising people in the 1960's. Another part concerns the ill-defined extent to which education and training in various countries has penetrated to broader groups in the population, and degrees of commitment to accepted social and economic values.

Interviews with creative people in England, the Low Countries, France, Germany, and Scandinavia suggest, however, that the same trend has been occurring, in varying measure, in all these markets. It seems reasonable to expect, therefore, that more and more controversy advertising will appear.

5

Public Means Publics

PUBLIC OPINION is, of course, composed of the definable opinions of multiple publics. Public controversy likewise involves participation of different groups, who together may be described as "the public" in the original Latin sense of the word—the people who have a choice in the political, social, economic, and legal processes of their society.

Except in cases of extreme emotionalism (where an advertiser wants passionately to reach "everybody"), or of media limitations (which force the advertiser to buy contact with many in order to reach a few), *controversy advertising is almost never addressed to the so-called "general public."* It is addressed to narrowly defined segments of the total available audience.

In contrast, *public-service advertising is almost always addressed to the broadest general public.* (Exceptions to this generalization, already cited, involve (1) free placement of public-service campaigns, as in the U.S., where the communicating organizations cannot exercise control and may experience odd distortions in audience exposure; and (2) paid insertions by governments, as in Scandinavia, where the effort to favor certain media, such as local newspapers, may likewise create an imbalance.)

When interviewed, the planners of major controversy advertising campaigns almost immediately make distinctions between the several audiences they intend to reach directly, and those whose coverage they consider an incremental benefit of the primary media strategy. In fact, the audiences reached may differ from the audiences which top management designated as targets. In part, this is owing to the difficulty of identifying specific segments of public opinion from the available demographic information about media audiences. Nonetheless, among the sophisticated controversy campaigns studied for this report, there is a consistency between the audiences targeted and the media chosen.

The patterns of audience selection that have emerged from the study suggest: (1) Target audiences chosen differ in terms of the three postures of controversy advertising defined earlier in this book. (2) Most controversy advertising is not intended to confound attackers, but to reach a) those who support (or are presumed to support) the point of view being presented, b) those most likely to accept and communicate the point of view to others, and c) those in the uncommitted category most inclined the passive acceptance of the advertised point of view.

These findings are relevant because they contradict the impression, fostered by people hostile to advertising of every kind, that corporations use controversy advertising to "swamp" and "drown" opposing opinion by placing the advertising in general-audience media and in media that reach adversary constituencies.

The opposition audience

The creative message of a controversy advertisement may appear to address directly a leader or member of the opposition. This is a creative ploy and, as will be explained further on, not very often used and not particularly successful in its results. The fact is that in terms of media used, controversy advertising is *very rarely* addressed directly to an audience opposed to its message.

This is as true for adversary campaigns—against California lettuce growers, New York slumlords, or Japanese corporations accused of pollution—as it is for corporation and association advertising against a strike action or in support of nuclear generation of electricity.

Thus, whatever the controversy, big U.S. corporations do not run advertising in *Ramparts, New Times,* the *Village Voice,* or *Rolling Stone* to state their point of view to a hostile audience. Nor do big British corporations use *Time Out, Private Eye,* or even *The Sun,* or French organizations use *Le Canard Enchaîné* or *Charlie Hebdo.* It is said that such media do not want and will not welcome such advertising. In fact, most would accept it, giving themselves the opportunity to reply editorially. It is also said that big advertisers are unwilling to give even the smallest advertising support to adversary media. This may be true, but interviews indicate that this is not the primary reason for not using them.

On the other side, even the best-financed adversary campaigns do not use the Establishment media either, whatever the country. Campaigns for preservation of the environment will use rock music radio stations rather than daily newspapers; posters, buttons, and bumper stickers rather than *Business Week, Handelsblatt,* or *France-Soir.* In fact, the counter-culture has in the past tended to create its own *ad hoc* media. (Like *Rolling Stone* in the U.S., those which survive seem destined slowly to cross over and join the Establishment as their editors gain in age and affluence.)

Why not talk directly to the opposition? Both sides agree that that is a waste of money. Chairman John Treasure of J. Walter Thompson in London, speaking before a recent *Times of London* seminar in Amsterdam, commented:

> Clearly, many of the critics from the Left have a set of beliefs which no corporate advertising or public relations could change except for the worse. . . .

Edwin Koupal, leader of a group called The People's Lobby, which took the adversary position in a California environmental controversy, told Prakash Sethi:

> One of our major mistakes in the campaign was that . . . we attempted to refute (the opposition) systematically in our campaign and in the process lost our audience and the opportunity to state our position. . . . One of the lessons learned from this campaign and successfully employed in later campaigns was "Keep controversy at a minimum. *Never debate.*" (S. Prakash Sethi, *op. cit.*)

It has already been pointed out that, from the analysis of IAA-developed case histories, a substantial amount of controversy advertising is generated, not from the bi-polar relationship between Establishment and counter-culture, but among Establishment members themselves to forward their particular positions and interests as the preferred alternatives in a controversy involving public choice. Much (if not most) of the volume of controversy advertising during the U.S. energy crisis did not revolve around defenses against public criticism of oil-company conduct, but advocacy of alternate solutions to ensure continuing supplies of energy at reasonable prices. The battles were between oil and coal, off-shore oil and landproduced oil, nuclear power generation and alternative means. In the U.K., key issues in a largely-concealed controversy seem to have concerned control of the benefits of North Sea oil and gas, and the right of foreign companies to have a share of the profits.

A final case where the general rule may not seem to apply involves "border-crossing" advertisements—those placed by a foreign country, company, or group in a domestic medium of a host country. Recent examples include (1) the full-page advertisement placed by President

Andres Perez of Venezuela in a September, 1974, issue of the *New York Times*, issuing an ultimatum to the U.S. concerning the ownership of petroleum companies; and (2) the advertisements placed (April, 1976) in the *New York Times*, the *Times* of London, and *Le Monde*, Paris, by a Venezuelan revolutionary group making demands on several countries and multinational companies. Were those not acts of direct confrontation through advertising?

Again, careful inspection suggests the contrary. The texts of both advertisements ask for support of, and appeal to, an audience presumed by the advertisers to be sympathetic to their causes. If the point that controversy advertising is rarely targeted directly at an adversary audience seems unduly stressed, it is because *most of the failure of communications in controversy advertising appears to result from the fact that the creators lose sight of the basic media targets and, in the creative execution of the advertising message, assume that they are really speaking to their opposition.*

The audience of supporters

Analysis of the media used in many different controversy campaigns shows that the media most used are those reaching audiences who already support or are sympathetic to the advertisers and their points of view. A good many advertisers will not agree with this. But, as was stated in one very large U.S. agency's presentation on corporate advertising, "Corporate advertisers often talk to themselves."

Selection of the target audience to reach supporters is similar to that of corporate image campaigns. Ralph Lewis, Editor and Publisher of the *Harvard Business Review*, has referred to the "five constituencies of the business firm: owners, employees, customers, general public, and government (national and local)." John Treasure of J. Walter Thompson offers a similar list of "four classic target groups for corporate advertising: employees, current and potential; shareholders, and the financial community; customers, suppliers, and competitors; and opinion leaders."

The key word is "constituency," those who are or can become members of a supporting group. Robert D. Lundy, Vice President for Advertising and Promotion of TRW, Inc., expressed the point at a recent seminar of the U.S. Association of National Advertisers: "Every corporation has a basic need to communicate with its constituents on issues important to them and to keep them informed of the corporation's actions and status. Constituents demand and deserve such communication. . . . Business fails to satisfy these communication needs at its peril. . . . I prefer the term 'constituent' to 'audience' because it implies responsibility to a group—it suggests that you should basically meet their need."

Harold Burson, Chairman of the large U.S.-based public relations firm, Burson-Marsteller, makes a similar comment: "The corporate cannot hold itself aloof from the political process. It must develop a *supportive constituency.*"

Examination of media schedules for the best-known controversy campaigns confirms this point. Mobil Oil's U.S. campaign has concentrated on the *New York Times* editorial page each Thursday, periodically experimenting with broader national coverage via daily newspapers, and in early 1976 shifting to add the *Wall Street Journal*, sections of the Sunday edition of the *New York Times*, and a number of other newspapers of national influence. Union Carbide, for the kinds of advertising it describes as "issue advertisements," uses only the *New York Times* and the *Washington Post*. American Electric Power has concentrated its advertising in four major UMS. business magazines, the three principal newsmagazines, plus the *New York Times*, *Wall Street Journal*, and the two Washington dailies, the *Post* and the *Star*. Similar findings emerge from analysis of media schedules for corporate controversy campaigns in the U.K. and elsewhere.

Some campaigns suggest exceptions to the overall strategy of making the natural constituents the major target for the corporation's point of view. American Electric Power has periodically used a long list of daily and weekly newspapers (69 dailies, 192 weeklies during the first year of the controversial campaign). In Great Britain, the Bristol Channel Ship Repairers' campaign was run prominently in the *Daily Mirror*, a newspaper of broad national coverage but blue-collar and Labor Party orientation. Does inclusion of such media suggest a broader effort, either toward non-constituents or actual adversaries?

In fact, both campaigns were addressed to natural constituents. The regional newspaper effort of American Electric Power was aimed at reaching *employees* and *customers* of the corporation's operating companies, in the service areas they cover. With nationalization of the company at issue, the Bristol advertisements in the *Mirror* were aimed at the workers on the shop floor who would be affected by the change to management by government. They were part of the natural constituency for a campaign centering on political action affecting their working conditions.

The influentials

The idea that most corporate campaigns are targeted at people who already agree has been difficult to accept for most of the corporations which, after all, are investing large sums of money in such advertising. They prefer to believe that they are winning people over, and that the people they are influencing themselves possess "influence." Thus, in describing their audience targets to researchers, the corporations repeatedly refer to reaching "influentials" or "initiators."

General Electric's corporate U.S. campaign (with considerable advocacy content) is thus aimed at "all adults, but particularly special-interest groups . . . opinion leaders, government and business people, educators." The published case history of a Chase Manhattan Bank campaign states that, "The audience was limited to people who could readily understand the problem and who could do something about it . . . top executives of major corporations and government officials."

In fact, what these advertisers appear to have in mind is groups within the general public which display characteristics similar to those of the company's natural constituents, and which, if still uncommitted, can be considered predisposed by all their other loyalties to accept the advertiser's point of view.

In terms of company participation in controversy, these audiences are consistently described as "up-scale," affluent, or "upward-mobile." Two characteristics are mentioned in the U.S. as distinguishing them from natural constituents: they are thought to be younger (Union Carbide speaks of a group between 18 and 34), and more technologically oriented (causing advertisers in the U.S. to include such media as *Psychology Today* and *Scientific American* in schedules otherwise dominated by business and news publications). Neither youth nor technological orientation has been cited in definitions of "influentials" described in the case histories from other countries. However, it has been noted that corporate campaigns in the U.K. often employ such publications as *New Scientist* and *New Society*, whose audiences are similarly oriented.

From the evidence, there is little indication that controversy advertising campaigns are ever aimed at "influentials" presumed to be on the opposite side. To clarify this anomaly, it is necessary to describe the three audiences thought by advertisers to have real influence on public opinion and actual decision-making:

1. *Journalists*—While controversy advertising no doubt serves to alert journalists to prospective news leads, there is little indication of controversy advertising aimed directly at them. They are generally considered by business as (a) inherently adversary or (b) completely committed to the corporate point of view. In either case, they are dealt with through the most personal means of public relations.

   Ironically, just such advertising to influence working journalists is called for by the conservative U.S. thinker, Irving Kristol. After disputing the ability of advertising campaigns to explain the American economic system to the general public, he calls on business to use advertising directed to the adversary journalist audience:

What has to be done, to set the record straight, is a public rebuttal—detailed, polemical, and sharply phrased, so as to challenge the reporter's (or newscaster's) professional integrity. And this rebuttal will have to take the form of paid advertising in that media which the reporter and his colleagues read.

2. *Educators and intellectuals*—Abundant educational materials are provided, usually as a public service, by corporations and public-interest groups, for the use of teachers discussing public issues with their students. The amount of material is greater at the primary and secondary level than at the university level, and more privately-provided material is available in the U.S. and U.K. than in most other countries.

   However, there has been little direct advertising by corporations in any country in measured media reaching educators themselves. This is apparently because this kind of approach—involving a signed, identified sponsor—would be considered suspect by this audience.

3. *Government officials and legislators*—Advertisements in the Anglo-Saxon countries, those sponsored both by business and by public-interest groups, regularly take the rhetorical position of speaking directly to responsible government officials and to the legislators concerned with specific controversies. Some effort is made to use media which the advertisers believe will be seen by these officials and legislators.

   The approach of such advertisements is, nonetheless, not to influence directly the judgment of the government figures supposedly addressed, but to signal to them the existence of a body of opinion of which they should be aware, and to induce them to give proper weight to the position which the advertisements advocate. At the same time, such advertisements regularly urge their constituents to communicate with the government officials so addressed. This function may be of more importance, in fact, than the ostensibly direct messages of appeal.

To sum up, the IAA survey material suggests that those to whom advertisers refer as "influentials" are in reality groups which, in terms of their general resemblance to natural constituents, logically should be constituents themselves. Advertisers believe that these people, not clearly committed, may choose some other alternative. The belief appears to be based on the assumption that these audiences are generally younger, and more oriented to science and technology. They correspond to the people described by Dr. Treasure as:

> middle-of-the-road opinion leaders and others who may be needlessly worried about certain problems and thereby encouraged to initiate or agree to policy measures which otherwise they would not have done so.

It is important to the advertiser to try to gain their support, and describing them as "opinion leaders" is, in itself, an effort to give them a sense of their own importance and to encourage their involvement. On the other hand, the real decision-makers and clearly definable "influentials"—journalists and other communicators, educators, government people—are generally reached through the "one-to-one" means of public relations, or not at all.

The uncommitted

For all practical purposes, advertisers planning controversy campaigns do not appear to consider, or address, some difficult-to-define groups of people who hypothetically have made no commitment. Interviews suggest that there are a large number of passive people in any given population who are unlikely to respond, whatever the stimulus; these are not classified as "uncommitted," however—simply excluded from planning.

The interlock between audience and posture

The reader of this report will have been struck by the similarities between the "natural constituency" for any given position in controversy, and the group referred to rightly or wrongly as "influentials," that is, people who strongly resemble supporters but have not given their allegiance to the cause.

The resemblance is so striking that Dr. Treasure comments that it is not worth making distinctions in terms of media planning between the categories being reached:

> I must confess my preference at the moment is to define the target audience for corporate advertising campaigns in terms of media audiences.

That is, it is easier to say, "we want to reach the kinds of people who read the *Times* of London, or *Nihon Keizai Shimbun*, or *Psychology Today*," than to do a demographic analysis of supporters and potential supporters, and then match this sketch to the demographics of the publications.

However, a significant difference turns up in the posture of the advertising addressed to these two groups. Advertising addressed to the committed supporters generally takes a defensive or strongly active stance, reinforcing their loyalty and building their enthusiasm and activity. "Influentials" are more prudently exposed to the "platform of fact" approach, as a general rule, and not exposed to a higher energy level except in periods or recognized crisis.

6

The Problems of Media Suitability and Access

THE DISCUSSION IN this report up to this point is based on empirical evidence from the most important examples of controversy advertising which we have been able to assemble. The ideas set forward are based on two assumptions:

1. That the advertisers employing this kind of communication know what media are best for their purposes.
2. That the best media are freely available to these advertisers.

Both assumptions are open to question. Emphasis has been placed on cases where the advertising seems successful and to the satisfaction of the advertiser. Still, it is apparent that in some cases, controversy advertising does not profit from the use of the most appropriate media vehicles, and it is worth finding out why.

The second assumption is, in fact, a matter of open controversy already. In varying degrees, campaigns and single advertisements concerned with controversy are barred from certain media: by law, by media industry agreement, by convention, or by sheer cost. In a number of countries, notably the U.S. and U.K., the advertising industry itself is divided over whether or not this kind of advertising should be allowed access to the electronic media, television and radio.

Media suitability for controversy advertising, as for any other advertising, depends on four factors:

1. *Audience coverage,* discussed in the previous section. In some countries, a particular medium is the only way to reach a target audience. In most countries, there is a choice between one medium and another; newspapers vs. magazines, print vs. television, for example, or various combinations of media may be selected.
2. *Cost.* Not simply cost efficiency, getting the target coverage at the best possible price, but raw unit cost as well. For a given budget, use of a certain medium may simply be out of the question. This is certainly the case for a number of controversy campaigns in the U.S., as far as use of television goes, and would probably be so in the U.K., Germany, France, Japan, and all other industrial nations, were television time available for the purpose.
3. *The nature of the message.* What the advertiser wants to say, not simply the basic thrust but the amount of content and detail to be included.
4. *Creative strategy.* Designed by the advertiser and those advising him.

Obviously, there is interplay among what the advertiser believes must be said, the ways his creative team would like to express it, and the media available to choose from. The next section of the report on "Alternative Message Patterns" explores creative strategies which appear in our study with frequency, indicating that the advertisers either believe they work well or prefer them for some other reason considered important enough to justify their repeated use.

With regard to the suitability of various media for controversy advertising, three statements are repeatedly made by both the advertisers and the creative people who design the advertising:

1. The nature of a controversy message intrinsically requires many words. This in turn supposedly requires print advertisements using long texts. Broadcast media (TV and radio) are more difficult to employ because of the length of the verbal message, problems of visualization on TV, and (over and above cost) the problem of maintaining the interest of the viewer/listener for a relatively long time.
2. Controversy advertising has to be prepared with extreme rapidity, to keep pace with the latest developments in any given situation. This eliminates media with long closing requirements, or those which require elaborate preparation of films, tapes, visual materials, plates, and the like. Hence, there is a tendency for advertisers to prefer the daily newspaper, with its fast closings, and radio, which permits almost instant modification of messages.
3. Controversy advertisers would make more use of television and radio, if they were allowed to do so. They believe that public-service

advertising in these media, and non-sponsored coverage of news events, have amply demonstrated the impact the broadcast media could bring to their advertising efforts. But, as already noted, they feel that they are often precluded from using these media, despite wanting to.

These three statements are not quite consistent with one another. Do controversy advertisements intrinsically require as many words as the manifesto-length examples would suggest? How often is the rapidity and flexibility of newspaper advertising really essential? For that matter, do magazines and television really require so much more time to get a controversy message on its way? And, if length of message and rapidity of getting the message out are so essential, why do some advertisers contradict themselves and say that they would use more television were it available to them?

Interviews suggest that the real explanation of the preference for lengthy newspaper advertisements stems from strong management involvement:

1. A tendency to long verbal clarifications.
2. Preference for newspapers, especially the financial pages, as the dignified environment for such messages.
3. A desire to present controversy opinions in an ambience and with the appearance of news.
4. Discomfort with choosing visual illustrations, with an inclination toward old-fashioned drawings and cartoons, or no visualizations at all.

It is worth noting that business's adversaries in many countries also tend toward the long-copy manifesto-length advertisement, apparently for the same reasons. So do governments, in the border-crossing advertisements they use to state their positions to foreign audiences, and even guerilla revolutionaries (for example, the 1976 Venezuelan kidnappers of a U.S. executive, who advertised their point of view in the *New York Times*).

Does controversy advertising have to be prepared with extreme rapidity to keep pace with developments and to meet media deadlines? It is certainly true that, if a parliamentary vote is scheduled for a certain date, then a balance must be struck between the time allotted to prepare the advertisements and the time required for the media to process and run them. But such cases are few. The urgency for preparing a controversy advertisement is for the most part internally generated within the advertiser organization.

Ad hoc creation of complete advertisements under pressure is not the only alternative. Other approaches include (a) development of a library of different advertising subjects, in anticipation of events, which can be adapted and finalized on short notice, and (b) preparation of a long-term, generalized "platform of fact" to reduce the time pressures involved and permit addition of an *ad hoc* statement of position to the campaign on short notice. (For example, the Union Carbide campaign in the U.S. employs this approach. See Case Examples.)

Finally, it is alleged, with justice, that in most countries the broadcast media either will not or are not allowed to accept advertising that explicitly takes sides in public controversy. In the U.K., a rule of the Independent Broadcast Authority forbids advertising directed toward "any religious or political end," or having "any relation to any industrial dispute," or showing "partiality as respects matters of political or industrial controversy or relating to current policy." While the IBA and its approval bodies are, in practice, in a position to exercise broad decision-making authority, it is quite clear that no broadcast advertising taking either the "defensive" or "aggressive" posture analyzed earlier in this study would be acceptable. Even the anti-inflation advertising prepared by the Government was sufficiently related to controversial public policy that its makers prudently designed it solely for print media in its first two phases.

In the U.S., outright "political" broadcast advertising is normally accepted by the media, though complex rules affect the amounts charged, time periods available, use of a candidate's voice, and the like. Operating individually, however, the acceptance units of the networks and stations refuse any sponsored message which would oblige them, under the Federal Communications Commission's Fairness Doctrine, to provide equal time for an opposing point of view. The broadcast media are so sensitive to the Fairness requirement that one network has even declined an advertiser's offer to pay for equal time for any opponent's message.

In other countries, broadcast time (other than that devoted to government-sponsored public-service commercials) is not available to commercial sponsors, or is limited to specific advertising categories which effectively exclude controversy commercials.

A more complex problem arises when broadcast transmitters located in one country are beamed to others. Thus far, such European commercial transmitters as Radio Monte Carlo, Radio Luxembourg, Europe No. 1, and others have not been employed for controversy advertising. The U.S.-Government-operated international radio stations, Radio Free Europe and Radio Liberty, like those of many other governments, frequently use a commercial-message format to convey messages of a clearly propaganda nature. To a lesser extent, propaganda messages are heard on government-controlled radio stations with a mixed commercial and public-service format (permitting a limited number of sponsored product commercials in a dominantly non-commercial program schedule) in the Middle East. For example, multinational transmissions from the Egyptian and Iraqi networks. Private sponsorship of political, social, and economic messages in these media is unknown.

Apart from these potentially troublesome international aspects, the basic questions are two:

1. Are broadcast media, particularly television, so inherently persuasive, or so subject to persuasive abuse, that in the public interest they should be barred from use in public controversy?
2. Given the opportunity, would advertisers abuse the broadcast media in promoting their points of view in public controversy?

These questions will not be answered here. President Edward Ney of Young & Rubicam International has taken a clear public position, answering "yes" to both questions so far as political advertising is concerned. The same reasoning would seem to apply equally to private sponsorship of social and economic positions. According to Mr. Ney, television "is basically incapable of doing justice to (political advertising) and is susceptible to ingenious mischief." The 30-second spot commercial is a "dangerously insufficient amount of time for a serious exposition of vital national issues. . . ." And "there is no self-regulatory control over false political promises, and no simple legal way to get an offending political spot off the air before the damage is done." Paradoxically, this most controversial category of controversy advertising, the specifically political, is not only allowed but heavily used on U.S. radio and television, whereas the advocacy use of television proposed by Mobil and other private sponsors is not accepted by these media.

These restrictions of access apply to the two postures, active and defensive, distinguished earlier. They do *not* apply to the third posture, the "platform of fact" approach, in which advertisements by choice of subject and presentation of factual content position the advertiser in the public's mind as having a right to a voice. As already indicated, this is essentially neutral communication, and it differs from corporate-image advertising only in intent and thus audience selection, and in selection of materials to be presented.

The "platform of fact" approach is being increasingly used and found acceptable by the broadcast media of the world. In Great Britain, Exxon has invoked the "Esso Tiger," and, with brilliant informative footage concerning North Sea operations, has effectively used commercial television to anticipate and overcome any possible problems. The company has thus established its claim to be involved in the exploitation of the new oil fields.

In the U.S., Union Carbide (using Young & Rubicam) has in a similar way explored company activities in product areas related to controversy, establishing its importance in these connections, and preparing the ground for discussion of controversial issues in daily newspapers. (See Case Example.) Philips of Eindhoven is running a worldwide campaign dealing with its products involved in controversial issues. Perhaps the longest-running campaign of this kind, also worldwide, was originated in 1915 by Caterpillar, major producer of agricultural and earth-moving equipment. (See Case Examples.)

In the U.S. this kind of television commercial (and related radio versions) is generally juxtaposed with programing that has a bearing on the issue, or on other matters of public controversy, thus providing a climate of interest in socio-economic affairs. In other countries, it is not so easy for an advertiser to arrange the positioning of a commercial with related program content, but commercial time is generally adjacent to the nightly news, giving approximately the same effect.

The cost of this approach is high. To achieve impact, the strategy must be applied consistently over time, so that the public may grow to accept, understand, and even anticipate the messages. Quick *ad hoc* response to current developments is precluded (just as it is in magazines).

However, going back to the two questions about using broadcast media for the purpose of controversy advertising, no one in countries where this approach has been tried has objected to it as abusive, despite airing of factual material clearly relevant to ongoing controversies. Regulation through the media themselves, self-regulatory bodies, and government organizations is adequate to maintain control, and corrections of factual material can be made.

The technique of engaging in controversy via broadcast media can be used in almost any country offering commercial time. In Germany, the Hamburg electric utility company (see Case Example) diverted time from some of its regular television schedule to explain nuclear production of energy in its region, using this approach to bring relief to a controversy rather than exciting one. The question may therefore be posed again: Would the advertisers who complain about lack of access to broadcast media use them if this technique were explained and its advantages pointed out?

While no generalization is possible, the interviews conducted suggest that many of those who say they would use television if they could, in fact would not. The amount of money required would inhibit some. The impossibility of making *ad hoc* ripostes at short notice would frustrate others. The difficulty of close management participation in the broadcast creative process would frustrate still others. Even in the case of Mobil in the U.S., where adroit funding of noncommercial programing has created a kind of cultural platform for the company, a number of commentators have pointed out that top management has seemed more comfortable taking an aggressive stance through its press advertisements.

7

Alternative Message Patterns

IT IS NOT the purpose of this report to provide a manual on how to do controversy advertising. Nor is it possible, here, to inventory all creative strategies.

However, the IAA survey and subsequent research have identified a number of patterns which are regularly employed as creative strategy. They illustrate, in varying measure, the points about controversy advertising thus far made.

Factual correction

The strategy of factual correction, in its pure form, reflects the conviction that a controversy is simply the product of misinformation or misunderstanding. The advertiser believes that clear, factual exposition if it does not eliminate disagreement, will at least consolidate support for his case.

Generally, the advertiser and his creative team perceive and communicate a note of urgency, over and above simple presentation of facts. This reflects their own emotional intensity about the importance of their message, and it tends to command attention. The approach is generally reinforced by offers of additional information: booklets, referral to an information service, or an invitation to response by telephone.

Immediate reaction

The decision to comment on a development, or reply to a statement or event, in "real time"—that is, within 24 to 48 hours—is a quite common strategy at the inception of a controversy. It reflects the advertiser's opinion that the issue is short-term and that it may be "nipped in the bud" by immediate action. The medium chosen is generally the newspaper, and the presentation of the advertising message is relatively unsophisticated.

However, some highly sophisticated and long-running campaigns have been designed in such a way that topical material can be integrated into them with great speed. The long-running Mobil Corporation messages for the position opposite the editorial page every Thursday in the *New York Times* are written against the newspaper's deadlines. In a somewhat different style, the Union Carbide issue advertisements in newspapers are designed to evoke recognition of the continuous "platform of fact" campaign running in magazines and on television.

One-time reply

Some advertisers believe that a single statement should be sufficient to bring opponents to reason, or to rally sufficient support to overcome them. In the cases where this supposition is naive, based on conviction in a righteous cause, the advertiser may pay only cursory attention to the communications qualities of the advertisement. Such advertising tends not to succeed, nor to be remembered.

However, there are excellent examples of one-time controversy advertisements which had striking success and almost indefinite memorability. Some are of extreme simplicity and employ unusual media such as lapel buttons or bumper stickers. Most share common characteristics: extreme simplicity of message, dramatic visualizations, and superior graphic treatment.

Warning to constituents

As already argued, the great majority of controversy advertisements are addressed to the supporters of the advertiser's point of view. Generally, this is implied rather than directly stated.

Warning them, even complaining about their inattention, is a recognized strategy which turns up in every kind of controversy advertising, whether one-time efforts or long-term campaigns, whether conservatively oriented or hyper-activist.

Mobilizing constituent support

Appealing to supporters and potential supporters to rally to a point of view amounts to taking the "warning" strategy one step farther. It is a more positive approach. More than informing them, it calls for some *specific action* such as writing to the company for literature, enlisting in organizations or movements, or writing, telephoning, and sending telegrams to government officials and legislators.

In their advertisements, adversaries of organized business have always prominently encouraged supporters to take direct action of this nature. Business, professional, and industrial associations have more discreetly encouraged the same thing. However, it has only been in recent years that individual business firms have gone beyond statements of policy to suggest what members of the public can do to have such policies implemented. Until recently, even these suggestions were generally stated discreetly at the end of an advertisement's text. But now, considerable numbers of business firms have "taken the gloves off" and are telling the public what they have to do, in boldface type.

The association as surrogate

The use of industry and professional associations to take collective stands in the name of their individual members has long been an accepted strategy in public controversies. It was a short step from public relations efforts directed at opinion leaders and governmental bodies to broader efforts, using advertising as the means of communication.

The advantages of using an association as the sponsor signing a controversy advertising campaign are numerous:

1. In many cases, such a campaign would be beyond the means of individual members
2. The advertising is prepared and supervised by the association's team of professional communications and legal advisers.
3. Consensus about policy questions is arrived at before the advertising appears, ensuring unanimity among the members.
4. The controversial point of view is attributed to the association, rather than the individual member. If real hostility and antagonism is aroused by the advertising, the association bears it collectively, and individual firms and persons are not directly affected.

The strategy of organizing a controversy campaign through an association has come under some criticism in recent years. The objections do not center on anti-trust or anti-cartel implications of such concerted action, but on the efforts of individual corporate members to avoid being identified while promoting self-serving policies under a cloak of anonymity. Of particular concern to the public are (a) *ad hoc* organizations, with resounding names, organized solely to sponsor such campaigns, and (b) associations grouping one or two very large members, together with a number of very small members, with resulting *de facto* control by the giants. In such cases, the value of the signature on the advertisements is undermined by questions about the true nature of the association.

In the U.S. and U.K., the trend appears to be away from the use of associations to take collective positions in controversy, and toward advertisements signed by individual firms. This is to some extent a reflection of policy disagreements noted earlier within industries in crisis, for example, among petroleum producers, other energy producers, transportation organizations and agencies.

Surrogate spokesmen

Advertisers have sought surrogates to present their policies in advertising messages. Several variations are increasingly popular:

1. Presentation of the opinions or endorsements—an interview, an essay, a speech transcribed—of prominent figures who agree with the sponsoring advertiser's point of view.
2. Presentation of a range of opinion drawn from a cross-section of the public, with the advertiser's position included as one of the alternatives advanced.

Direct counterattack

Advertisements which state the opposing view and then attack it are fairly rare. Two risks are entailed: the statement of the opponent's case may be perceived as more credible than that of the advertiser's, and the tone employed in the advertisement may be too defensive, or too aggressive, and may thus alienate audience members who are otherwise inclined to agree. Techniques of reducing these kinds of risks include the use of humor, personalization, and provocative questions that involve the audience.

Rational explanation

The "rational explanation" strategy involves presenting both sides of the question, explaining the trade-offs involved, and then presenting the advertiser's point of view. Unlike the direct counterattack, the opposing viewpoint is presented neutrally, not in a manner intended to make it appear weak. Every effort is made to present the alternatives in a fair manner, with the conclusion drawn in favor of the advertiser's point of view, or, possibly, left hanging.

This strategy is difficult to execute. Some advertisers feel compelled to attempt it, because of their opponents' attacks on the amounts of money they have available to present their points of view. One manner of handling the approach is to offer space or time to the opponent, to be freely used to state the opposition viewpoint. For example, Mobil Oil Corporation has offered to underwrite television time for the use of its critics, if the U.S. networks will allow its own messages to be presented. Most proposals of this sort appear to break down as a result of differences over ground rules for the opponent's participation. Without opponent participation, the two-viewpoint rational explanation obviously leaves the credibility of the advertiser open to question.

Contribution of audience members

The most extreme form of audience participation is political action. On the adversary side, this has meant advertisements demanding consumer strikes against the purchase of grapes, lettuce, and wines; protest marches against nuclear energy installations; and protest action by workers (exhorted in radio advertising from Mexican stations to Chicanos in Southern California, for example). On the corporate side, calls for letter-writing campaigns and efforts to influence voting patterns have been made.

The shortcoming of such direct appeals for action is that they succeed only with a minority of supporters, and they generally fail to gain the interest of potential supporters, who "don't want to get involved."

Somewhat less pointed campaigns have recently been developed which invite the general public (that is, interested people) to submit their ideas. Perhaps the most ingenious recently developed in the U.S. is the Atlantic Richfield campaign, in which the public was first invited to submit ideas about the future of transportation, then those people participating were turned into surrogate spokesmen whose comments were used to explore the energy situation. (See Case Example.)

Information base

In an earlier section of this report, the posture of establishing a "right to a voice" in a given public controversy was discussed. We attempted to distinguish this posture, and the "platform of fact" needed to justify it, from conventional corporate-image advertising intended solely to enhance reputation and good will.

In many countries, there has been a shift in corporate advertising from conventional descriptions of products and projects to emphasis on current preoccupations of the public. The shift is often motivated not so much by desire for involvement in controversy, as by the vague desire to be in step with the fashion. In the U.S. a 1975 survey by the Association of National Advertisers of 114 large companies found that about 30% of their corporate advertising centered on questions of the environment, energy, and private-enterprise economics.

The percentage of such advertising—raising the issues of controversy, preparing for controversy, but not embarking upon a course of controversial advocacy—purposefully undertaken is hard to calculate. That this kind of factual presentation is a deliberate strategy on the part of a number of advertisers is not subject to doubt. The examples of Union Carbide in the U.S., and Tate & Lyle in the U.K., have been mentioned. While the information in such campaigns is factual, creative efforts are given free rein. Such "platform of fact" campaigns are generally characterized by long-term planning, continuity, access to all kinds of media, and a high degree of professionalism in their preparation. Subjects focus on how a company's products and activities link it to socioeconomic questions currently in the news, and how the company has an effect on the life of the individual.

Advertising of this nature appears to have intrinsic interest to its audience and is reported to be highly popular. It also tends to win praise from advertising professionals, and often to be perceived as public-service advertising.

Generic controversy and individual product advertising

Products created to exploit technology in order to offer specific benefits may be inherently controversial at the time they are conceived. They may become controversial later on as the result either of environmental or other effects, or shifts in social or economic priorities.

Makers of such products, assuming they are not withdrawn, have four options: (a) cease advertising the product; (b) continue promoting it but in a neutral manner, making no reference to its controversial aspects; (c) undertake a separate campaign to state the company's point of view concerning the value of the product and justify its continued sale and use; (d) integrate mention of the controversial aspects into conventional product promotion.

There are certain product categories in which, once controversy has been raised, it is impossible to continue advertising in a neutral manner, and efforts to isolate the controversial aspects into a separate campaign simply don't work. In such cases options are limited to suspending the advertising altogether, or blunting the controversial aspects in an attempt to turn them to the favor of the product.

Such cases generally include products or services whose use conflicts with traditional or conventional patterns of behavior:

> The example of condom advertising—medically approved as a means of preventing transmission of epidemic disease, but disapproved by many as a mechanical means of birth control, and also disapproved as a subject for public discussion—has already been mentioned.
>
> Promotion of certain tabooed foodstuffs to improve nutrition (for example, milk in certain African countries) is *per se* controversial.
>
> Discussion of the treatment of venereal disease, in public-service campaigns sponsored by government in some countries, is resisted by the media, and in the U.S. has to be sponsored as paid controversy advertising.
>
> A supersonic commercial airliner, advertising its claims for speed and low noise, by such action tacitly counterattacks its critics in worldwide media.

Exploitation of controversy for sales purposes

Occasionally an advertiser will attempt to tie a product into a fashionable controversy, in the hope of increasing its sales. When it is deliberate, this may be viewed as a cynical strategy, since it attempts to exploit public concern for selfish, short-term purposes.

Thus, according to Prakash Sethi, a number of U.S. companies have tried to "make light of the public's concern for pollution and the environment by treating it as a gimmick . . . in an attempt to boost the sales of their products." Dr. Sethi lists a surprising number of companies cited by the Council for Economic Priorities as having so done, including major cigarette manufacturers, beverage producers, etc.

However, most cases of this found by the IAA survey tend to be less cynical than naive. They include advertisements linking restaurant menu prices to concern about inflation and free-enterprise economics, headlines about energy and nutrition questions which are not discussed in the copy, and the like.

Such advertisements, whether cynical or naive, undermine the credibility and attention-value of advertising displaying genuine social and economic concern.

8

Critical Elements of Execution

THIS SURVEY, with its relatively limited base, must necessarily be cautious in drawing conclusions or making generalizations. The case examples presented, the other examples studied, and wide-ranging interviews all point to a number of critical elements which affect how an audience receives any controversy advertising campaign.

Analysis of these elements must be prefaced with a general comment. The opinion of many qualified advertising men is that most controversy advertising is not very well done. Pressed to explain why the campaigns are of poor quality, judgments seem to divide between those who find the work too amateurish, and those who think it altogether too professional, in the slick sense.

John O'Toole, of Foote, Cone & Belding, comments on the failure to employ the most basic communications techniques:

> I have to register some disappointment with the way it (advocacy advertising) has been approached by most companies . . . throwing a bunch of numbers at (the reader). . . . Talking about your earnings and your costs (means nothing to him) . . . but talking to him about *his* costs might . . . about *his* needs and *his* home and *his* family might. . . .

John Treasure of J. Walter Thompson declared in Amsterdam that:

> In my experience the more serious errors in advertising are committed by doing the wrong thing well rather than by doing the right thing badly.

The campaigns reported as successful in their communications impact share four elements which were apparently critical to their being well conceived and working effectively.

Objectivity

Harry Darling of the U.S. Association of National Advertisers has suggested that any campaign of this nature is not undertaken simply in the public interest, but in hopes of specific benefit to its sponsor as well. The most admired campaigns are those which manage to keep this factor of self-interest from altering or interfering with the facts and judgments on which the advertising must be based.

This is a surprisingly serious problem. Arthur Duram, of Fuller & Smith & Ross, noted in 1972 that a company and an agency might have collaborated successfully for years on effective product advertising, but "put the same company and agency to work on a new project called 'corporate advertising' and years of disciplined experience melt away in the strange joy of pure 'sloganeering.' " Close involvement of top executives who have not previously taken a direct role in communications can be a factor. As Irving Kristol points out,

> Hardheaded executives really do believe that if they show some dramatic pictures of corporate activity, with the accompanying assurance that "we're involved" or "we're concerned" or "we're working for America" or whatever—that this will somehow persuade people to think well of that particular corporation, and of business in general. The notion is absurd. All such institutional (corporate) advertising collapses into one glossy blur and has no effect whatsoever on anyone. Well . . . it does serve to pacify the anxious chief executive, and to gratify his ego, too. Perhaps this therapeutic effect is worth the money expended.

It is certainly true that corporate executives, like the leaders of adversary groups, are often convinced that they are not involved in persuasion, but are simply providing factual information so compelling that right-minded people must of necessity accept it and support the position advanced. This high degree of conviction, not put in a context of rigorous objectivity, apparently can interfere with many aspects of the communications process.

Exploitation of communications as an opportunity for personal ego gratification has often been criticized. This tendency appears fairly often in controversy campaigns, calling to mind David Ogilvy's well-known lines:

> When the client moans and sighs,
> Make his logo twice the size.

If he still should prove refractory,
Show a picture of the factory.
Only in the gravest cases
Should you show the clients' faces.

Harold Burson, writing on the practical aspects of managing corporate campaigns, feels constrained to comment that not all top executives are photogenic or good personalities for television.

Techniques used to foster objectivity in appraising the communications need in a controversy are discussed in the next section of the study, "Organizing to Carry Out the Campaign."

Credibility

It is elementary that the advertising message in a controversy advertisement must be *believable*.

The first prerequisite is that what the advertisement says must correspond to the facts publicly available. Irving Kristol, discussing the problem of a corporation forced to defend itself against slander, argues that it should act "with the indignation and forcefulness that we expect from an innocent victim of slander." But, he goes on, "Obviously, to do this, a corporation has indeed to be innocent, or, to put it more reasonably, at least not guilty as charged. . . ." If something is really "wrong," then the employment of controversy advertising may be counter-productive.

Recently, a large international chemical manufacturer was preparing an important corporate campaign with controversial aspects, linking its employees' well-being with the need for corporate profits. Investigation of pollution conditions at a production facility formerly controlled by the corporation revealed serious health hazards. Critics questioned the corporation's real concern for the employees in this supplier's plant. Rather than confront an apparent conflict between newspaper reports and the position taken in the advertistements, the corporation withdrew the campaign and revised the creative strategy.

Even minor detail, if challenged, can seriously undermine credibility. An example is a campaign prepared for a coal producers association in the U.S. It was revealed by the *Wall Street Journal* that a coal miner portrayed in the advertisements as "man of the year" was actually a vice president of the association's advertising agency, serving as a model. Press comment subjected the association to ridicule.

Exaggeration can also be risky. *Business Week*, commenting on the American Electric Power advertisements during the oil crisis, pointed out that "some of them seriously overstate the problems. . . . They blemish what is otherwise a legitimate effort to broaden public understanding." John O'Toole commented on this same aspect of the campaign, which he felt depicted as a villain "the oil-rich, insidious Arab sheik. The tactic reminds me of the fat, grasping U.S. capitalist we used to see caricatured in Russian journals. It's too facile a simplification for today's reader."

Another component of credibility is described, for lack of a better expression, as "tone of voice." This refers to the emotional cues through which the advertising message seeks to attract the attention and establish empathy with the audience. While these cues can be non-verbal, most examples collected in the IAA research concern the language and style of textual material.

The advertiser and the people he employs to design the message obviously seek a particular "tone," generally one of sincerity, but which can range from urgency and excitement to solemnity and concern. Exceptions occur in situations of crisis, where the pace of events may provoke a tone of extreme emotionalism on the part of the advertiser.

Bruce McDonald, Vice President of Needham, Harper & Steers responsible for the ITT corporate campaign in England (see Case Examples), commented that one of the ground rules for that campaign was that "it could not be crisis-oriented." John O'Toole comments in sorrow that "Many advocacy advertising programs are born out of crisis. . . . Acceptance, to say nothing of credibility, is hard to achieve under such circumstances."

When the intended tone is achieved to the satisfaction of the advertiser, it is nevertheless possible that (a) the tone adopted is miscalculated, and offends the audience addressed, or (b) that the audience perceives a different tone and different information than the advertiser expected. (The phenomenon of misperception is well known to product advertisers, who spend substantial sums on qualitative research to find out what consumers "play back" after exposure to advertising.)

Criticism of "tone of voice" is quite outspoken in the U.S., somewhat less so in the U.K. and elsewhere. The tone of counter-culture advertising is regularly denigrated by its own supporters, who deplore its jargon, emotionalism and hysterical scare tactics. Corporate advertising is similarly subjected to close scrutiny by people well-disposed to its objectives. Particularly subject to criticism in controversy advertising is a tone of outrage, generally combined with an evocation of austerity. This tone, apparent in several of the examples included in this volume, has been referred to as the "let's get mad together" approach. It invites the audience to participate in the advertiser's concern about social and economic problems they might prefer to disregard. Adam Hanft, writing in *Madison Avenue* (July, 1975), argued that "In many cases we would do well to avoid heavily freighted advertising with allusions to, and imagery of economic malaise. . . . When reality becomes a crushing burden, nobody wants to be reminded of the weight." Similarly, an executive of a Belgian business publication attacked an international company's advertising about nutrition during an interview. The advertisement was in "poor taste," she said, because it used a shocking photograph of a starving child.

The effort to sound reasonable has also elicited criticism. Columnist Tom Wicker, writing in the *New York Times*, attacked a number of the petroleum companies' attempts to explain their positions, referring to their efforts as "pious, self-serving, devious, mealymouthed, self-exculpating, holier-than-thou, positively sickening oil-company advertisements in which these international behemoths depict themselves as paragons of virtue embattled against a greedy and ignorant world."

Another factor in rejection of controversy advertising is a built-in prejudice against anything that hints of persuasion, even among the people who support the point of view presented or generally believe in the position function of advertising. Barry Day of McCann-Erickson comments:

> In the hubbub of the consumer marketplace, of course, the difficulty of getting heard remains, no matter who you are and no matter how worthy your cause. A public inured to communications techniques is skeptical of any kind of sell.

Prakash Sethi suggests that, by their tone of voice, some controversy campaigns *invite* hostile reactions. He quotes the comment of Martin Fitzwater of the U.S. Environmental Protection Administration that the American Electric Power campaign (about the energy crisis and environmental pollution) "was of great advantage to us. The ads gave us a chance to make our case before an audience we otherwise did not have. . . . The people who saw these ads and then read the editorials probably thought that big business was trying to (sabotage the) public interest."

The choice of media can also affect credibility. While media selection is subject to rational decisions, conventional ideas about the appropriate medium for a controversy message may in fact misfire. For example, the preoccupation with newspaper advertisements has been criticized by Barry Day, writing in *Advertising Age:*

> So the argument goes, the no-nonsense, take-it-or-leave-it quality of the newspaper ad shows that you have nothing up your sleeve. The newspaper cannot lie!

But, in fact, adverse comment in adjacent newspaper articles can completely vitiate the advertiser's argument.

If the nature of the message is conspicuously inappropriate for the medium, overall credibility is jeopardized no matter what the medium's orientation. Calls for mobilization of general public opinion in a demonstration of practical democracy seem out of place in publications whose circulations reach only top management and wealthy individuals. Likewise, advertisements addressing the housewife about a company's concern for her interests do not ring true in magazines and newspapers chiefly aimed at financial analysts and bankers.

Audience receptivity

It is a truism of psychology that the attitudes a person already possesses, combined with the information already available to him, affect how he will perceive new information. An African native, exposed to an industrial plant without prior conditioning, will understand very little and even will *notice* very little.

This principle has limited relevance to much of conventional advertising, since most product promotion is addressed to experienced consumers and is concerned with developing preference for one product over another, within a context of shared audience knowledge about the product category. The principle is relevant when altogether new product concepts are to be launched. Established attitudes have to be altered, and new habits and use patterns developed.

A controversy, by definition, confronts the audience with an issue or conflict which may already have been latent in its subconscious, but of which the audience is now made consciously aware. One side in the controversy may seek to preserve and reinforce existing attitudes and behavior in the atmosphere of heightened sensitivity and stress to which the audience is now exposed. Other factions may seek to modify existing behavior patterns, or to substitute wholly new attitudes and actions.

Generally, the role of advertising in controversy is to reinforce existing behavior, not to teach new patterns. If the audience is not prepared for it, advertising to change attitudes in a controversial situation can be counter-productive. Even highly objective and credible advertising seems to have been rejected or discounted in many cases because of lack of audience receptivity.

Discussing the way in which some corporate campaigns are "born out of crisis," John O'Toole has described the dismay of the audience when "a company that has never established its identity with the reader is suddenly confronting him with its point of view about an important and controversial issue." Inadequate preparation leaves the audience unable to receive or even perceive the advertising message. It is difficult for many advertisers to understand that even their most logical supporters may possess a very low level of awareness of what is to the advertiser a burning issue of crisis proportions.

Similar problems arise when the advertiser, engrossed in his own arguments, fails to understand the context in which the audience frames a particular advertisement or campaign. An argument to justify profits is taken one way during a period of stable prices, but perceived quite differently during rapid inflation, for example.

A continuing program of communications—such as those run in the U.S. by Mobil Corporation and Union Carbide, and worldwide by Philips of Eindhoven, Siemens, and others—overcomes the problem of correct timing through sustained effort to maintain audience receptivity. (This is expensive, and success is not necessarily ensured.) The Tate & Lyle "Mr. Cube" campaign in the U.K. (see Case Examples) demonstrates that audience receptivity can persist over time and can be restored to a high level relatively rapidly.

The cases studied in this book suggest, at the very least, the need for monitoring audience receptivity through research prior to, during, and after any extensive campaign of controversy advertising. As a general rule, however, these steps have so far been taken infrequently. (See "Measurement of impact" in the following section.)

Definition of objectives

Many of the foregoing observations in this report suggest that, if much controversy advertising is of poor quality, this is the result not alone of the sensitive nature of the issues discussed, but of poor management of the advertising task as well.

Many reports were received about the tendency of advertisers to *assume* that they have sufficiently defined their objectives. Gary Thorne of the London *Times* comments that "Frequently corporations do not have clearly defined company policies . . . and spend their time papering over the cracks." He adds that "If the objective of the company is false, the advertising will be false."

In an effort to bring discipline to the task of establishing objectives and measuring performance, some business theorists have advocated use of a "social audit," an analysis of a company's socio-economic contributions and definition, in terms of accepted norms, of what its immediate and long-term objectives should be. This procedure permits construction of an acceptable idealistic base for future corporate conduct, including communications in relation to society. Adoption of a corporate "code of conduct" has much the same function as the social audit.

In the last analysis, the advertiser should clearly define the goals to be reached in a situation of controversy, and determine what role, if any, advertising is to play.

9

Organizing for the Campaign

MANY ADVERTISERS have expressed some reluctance to reveal for this study the way they organize and the procedures they follow in developing and executing this kind of advertising. Their general position is that this is "proprietary information." Their concern seems to focus on three problems: (a) that examination of how a company arrives at public statements of its position in a specific controversy could be interpreted in some damaging way by adversaries or competitors, (b) that the decision-making process involved might be taken as typical or representative of all decision-making activities in the company, and (c) that careful scrutiny of such operations by both government and financial sectors would be invited.

Nevertheless, enough companies have been generous with their time and information that their activities can be described in detail in our case examples. The texts have been cleared by them to ensure complete accuracy.

The same caution has been shown by government organizations which have, under various circumstances, become engaged in controversy advertising as distinct from their normal public-service communications.

Public relations firms, which have traditionally handled both direct communications, including controversy advertising, and indirect communications for their clients, also display caution about specific cases, although they are more than willing to discuss theoretical points about procedures.

Advertising agencies and specialist units such as creative consultants and "boutiques," media buying services, and other types of independent advisers have shown themselves much more eager to talk about their work. However, few records have been kept, few agencies have extensive experience in this kind of advertising, and those that do are understandably cautious not to issue any information that might be prejudicial to their clients.

On the adversary side, public-interest agencies and other groups have been more than willing to discuss how they proceed, in the quest for further publicity for the causes which concern them. In fact, most of these groups are quite small, experience constant turnover in leadership and personnel, and generally operate on an *ad hoc* basis. They therefore have little to contribute to understanding how the process can best be managed.

Organizational structure and relationships

There is no preferred way of organizing for a controversy advertising campaign. There are several reasons for this.

First, the number of firms explicitly and consciously sponsoring controversy advertising is limited. While public-interest groups by definition are engaged in controversy, there is a not surprising diffidence on the part of corporations to admit it. Thus, many of the campaigns in countries like the U.S., U.K., Germany, and Scandinavia which contain elements of controversy are regarded by the companies sponsoring them as public-service or corporate-image advertising. The points of view expressed are so intrinsic to these companies' normal activities that it takes an effort on their part to see the advertising as a form of advocacy.

Second, as has already been pointed out, while explicit use of controversy advertising is as old as advertising itself, the level of this activity has until recently been very low. Other means of communications, such as use of political forums and public relations, have been preferred.

Third, partly because of the unfamiliarity, partly because the need has been perceived only gradually, most firms had little idea of how to proceed, or where to turn for assistance. The conventional advertising agency often had scant experience *as an organization* with this kind of advertising, although individual agency people frequently did.

The conventional public relations firm, on the other hand, possessed experience in this kind of communication but had little or no experience in advertising and did not possess the functioning service groups required to handle the physical production and placement of the advertising. The corporations themselves rarely had communications staffs large enough or specialized enough to handle such work.

A fourth reason for lack of organization in controversy advertising is the way in which a firm makes the commitment to follow this course. While the suggestion and impetus may come from almost anywhere in the firm, the actual decision to commit funds is taken—almost without exception—at the highest corporate level. The decision involves not just whether or not to do this kind of advertising, but also the lines of policy to be followed, the amount of money to be committed, and *who* in or outside the firm are to be assigned the responsibility.

In most companies (except some large consumer-goods firms) top management is not in direct or frequent contact with day-to-day advertising operations, and for the most part advertising executives do not participate in corporate policy-making. The top management official who takes the decision to run advertising which reflects corporate policy does not normally associate this communications assignment with line advertising tasks. He usually considers it an assignment for the legal or public affairs staff, or an activity to be handled directly at corporate staff level, even if this requires creation of a special unit.

The third and fourth factors—lack of the special capability needed to provide this kind of advertising, and top management's role in deciding, on the basis of little experience, to whom the task should be assigned— appear, according to the IAA interviews, to have had two consequences:

1. In a number of countries including the U.S., firms that might otherwise have undertaken controversy advertising have not done so, fearing amateurism in technical execution and possible embarrassment.
2. In most cases where controversy advertising has been undertaken, the campaigns have been organized and structured on an *ad hoc* basis.

There is some evidence from the interviews that the advertising executives within the firm, and the firm's advertising agencies, may be called in long afterward. The implication is that at first, product-oriented advertising experience and the emphasis on selling are regarded as inappropriate to the controversy task, and even that advertising professionalism is distrusted as too "slick" for the purpose.

There are four basic patterns for organizing controversy advertising:

1. *Assignment in-house.* The corporation itself exercises all responsibility for the development of the advertising, including complete creative development. When this course is taken, it almost always involves top management in the creation of a special advertising unit, rather than delegation of the assignment to the existing advertising structure.
2. *Assignment to public relations.* Controversy advertising is seen as a public relations or corporate public affairs activity, and is assigned,

through the corporate public relations staff, to an outside public relations counsel. (The public relations firm may thereafter, if necessary, subcontract execution and placement of the advertising to agencies and suppliers.) Until the early 1970's, assignment of such projects to the public relations function was the characteristic pattern for large corporations in the U.S. and Western Europe. The large public relations firms responded by creating "social affairs" units specializing in such areas as consumerism and the environment.

3. *Assignment to creative boutiques.* There is a strong tendency in some countries to assign controversy advertising to creative boutiques, small organizations which emphasize speed, flexibility, and innovativeness. The reasons for this choice are many: (a) many are well known for their work on public-service campaigns, or the involvement of their principals in social and political movements; (b) their small size protects confidentiality; (c) absence of bureaucratic structure provides flexibility and speed; (d) company top management can work directly with the boutique principals on the creative development.

4. *Assignment to a full-service agency.* Employing a conventional full-service agency appears to be a growing trend, in recognition of the need for consistency of effort and long-term commitment to this kind of advertising. Corporations now appear likely to turn to a full-service agency if (a) there is a close personal relationship between top executives in both organizations, (b) the agency has a specialized unit for corporate advertising, and/or (c) the agency has built a strong reputation for creativity, often in voluntary public-service campaigns. The larger the expenditure, the more likely the employment of a full-service agency, even though the conception of the advertisements may be retained wholly or partly within the corporation. When a controversy campaign is international in scope, it is likely that an agency with the capability of multinational coordination will be brought in.

Initiation of activity

While ideas for controversy advertising can come from anywhere in the company, interviews suggest that the company advertising departments rarely are a source. Their role is to respond to management initiative. On the other hand, public relations units are regularly a source of ideas.

The decision to undertake controversy advertising *always* comes from management: Chairman, President, Chief Executive Officer, or Chief Operating Officer. Members of the Board may also share in the decision. (The exception would be the case of a largely autonomous division or subsidiary, usually located in another country, where the chief executive might be authorized to initiate a controversy campaign.)

Development of material and plan

In situations where organizing for controversy advertising is *ad hoc* and there has been little experience, the planning tends to be haphazard and dependent on the attention available from top management. This is reported as leading to long periods of delay and indecision, followed by abrupt commitment and crisis production of materials. There is divided opinion about the results: Some advertising professionals think that hasty production results in amateurish creative execution and unimaginative use of media. Others argue that a sense of urgency inspires enthusiasm and greater effort, and thus produces more striking advertising. Different situations no doubt produce different results.

Large advertising agencies are now attempting to develop a controversy advertising capability, in the belief that this will ensure quality, economy, and continuity of agency and client procedures. Advertisers who have assigned this kind of work to full-service agencies report that they are generally satisfied with agency performance.

Approval stages and levels

There is an important difference, in organizing for controversy advertising, between the full-service agency on one hand and small in-house, boutique, or public-relations groups on the other. Where a full-service agency is employed, the advertising is always subject to clearly-defined levels of approval, in both agency and advertiser organizations. In one reported case, every advertisement produced was subject to 14 separate stages of approvals by both client and agency, before the advertising was released to the media. Exceptions are nevertheless made in urgent situations, where advertisements must be produced on short notice.

Where a small group is employed, approval is concentrated either at the top management level, or rests with an individual or committee to whom top management has delegated full authority and responsibility to take decisions.

Measurement of impact

Measuring the impact of controversy advertising is possibly the most disputed area in this study. Some advertisers report using syndicated services or doing research themselves to measure the attitudes of various audiences to controversial issues before and/or after they have undertaken controversy advertising campaigns. However, they scrupulously avoid any claims that a shift in public opinion about broad issues can be directly traced to their campaigns, and they generally take the position that the information about such shifts is confidential. We can only report that any research results given us have been favorable, indicating that a controversy campaign was successful in one or more of its objectives.

Some advertisers report using focus-group interview techniques in the development of creative approaches, and also using both small and large samples to measure attitudes toward the company—its point of view or, more frequently, its activities.

Most companies report that they have not made any effort to pre-test the effectiveness of their controversy campaigns, and that they have not attempted to measure the impact of the advertising following its appearance.

Why have most advertisers *not* attempted to measure the impact of campaigns usually involving large expenditures and, often enough, their corporate reputations? The reasons have to do with methodology and organization:

1. *Methodology.* Some researchers take the position that it is impossible to measure the impact of controversy advertising because (a) there are too many communications variables, or (b) the research input contaminates the experimental situation. That is, the asking of questions about the subject prior to exposure to the advertising creates an awareness and possibly affects attitudes which in turn condition the perception of and reaction to the advertising when it appears.

   These objections are made generally to attempts to measure the defensive and aggressive postures of controversy advertising, which seek to stimulate some specific kind of action. In the kind referred to as "platform of fact," such objections are said to be less applicable. It is possible, according to opinion researchers, to measure change in awareness about a company's involvement in or commitment to an issue. However, very few companies engaged in controversy advertising employ such research, while, paradoxically, companies using *non*controversial corporate image campaigns are reported to do so systematically.

2. *Organization.* Several organizational reasons have been cited in interviews to explain why controversy advertisers do not attempt opinion research:

   Top management, because it is not sufficiently close to research procedures, will not understand or will tend to misinterpret shifts in attitude scores and scaling procedures.

Unfavorable results reported to top management could have serious repercussions within the company, owing to the high level of emotional involvement often present.

Research scores reflecting favorable results could, in the long run, pose problems by encouraging researchers to base measurement of future advertising impact on the first round of successful scores.

A number of executives interviewed admit that these objections are not technically valid. However, they point out that, from a practical point of view, attempts at impact measurement might have such negative repercussions internally as to discourage use of any controversy advertising.

Some sponsors of the campaigns studied (notably American Electric Power, Tate & Lyle, the German electricity group) have sought to use both spontaneous and prompted audience responses as quantitative measures of impact. American Electric Power has included coupons in its advertising, inviting readers to respond in favor of or against its position. Other advertisers offer booklets or reprints, and "key" the advertising so that responses can be traced to specific advertisements and media. The companies using these techniques tend to place great emphasis on them as indicating the amount of impact of the advertising. Opinion research and direct-response specialists consulted comment that, where "attention-value" and "positive-attitude" are under study, such responses provide a rough-and-ready measurement. They maintain that if negative reaction is important to measure, spontaneous write-ins, coupon returns, and even requests for documentation do not provide reliable indications, since people hostile to the company's point of view generally do not respond.

10

Controversies About
Controversy Advertising

IN THE COURSE of the research for this book, several questions emerged which, even in the context of controversy advertising, are notably controversial. Following are the important areas of dispute about this advertising.

Border-crossing advertising

With the exceptions already noted (some radio "spill," some national publications with significant circulation in other countries, some truly "international media"), the advertising media of the world are directed to national audiences and serve national markets or, better put, the aggregate of markets within national boundaries.

The bulk of advertising which appears in a country is placed from within that country. There has always been a certain amount of advertising placed or financed from across national frontiers, generally to support products imported. In developed countries, such international advertising budgets usually bolster the available national budgets for product advertising, or are used for corporate advertising requirements, not only image but financial and legal announcements. In developing countries, advertising often originates abroad, because the infrastructure for professional creation and placement locally is viewed as inadequate.

Border-crossing paid political communications (technically speaking, "white propaganda," or propaganda whose source is identified) have historically been shunned by national media, as well as by the commercial international broadcast media. Except for mention of product origin (the "image" of national specialty often serving as a guarantee of uniqueness and quality), border-crossing product and company advertising was nearly always devoid of explicit involvement in international political questions. This is no longer true.

International politics and international economics have clearly merged since the conclusion of the Second World War. A great deal of advertising across borders at the present time is concerned with economic and social questions, even cultural questions, which formerly were discussed and negotiated behind closed diplomatic doors or publicized through news reports. Much of this advertising, perhaps all, qualifies under our definition of controversy advertising.

The great bulk of the new border-crossing advertisements stems from controversy originating in the developing world and is placed by governments, government-supported national associations, and economic alliances representing groups of developing countries—OPEC, for example.

Other border-crossing advertising includes campaigns such as those by the Japan Fisheries Association and the South African Olympics Committee. It is the purpose of these economically "developed countries" to communicate government policy through the commercial media of the North American-Western European markets.

So far, there has been very little border-crossing advertising from the developed countries in Third World media which can be identified as controversy advertising. The only notable example found in our research was a single advertisement run in 1966 in the Egyptian national newspaper, *Al Ahram*, to argue the important economic and social role played by the Coca Cola Company in the Arab countries. The advertisement appeared a month before an important Arab League meeting but failed to forestall a boycott of the company's products and closing of its plants. Further research may identify advertising by foreign owners in developing countries to resist expropriation of their properties.

The origins of Third World advertising to present arguments to the economically developed countries can probably be traced to two earlier phenomena:

> The aggressive use of public relations, including paid advertising, to promote certain commodities and to enhance national prestige during the immediate postwar period. In some cases the advertising was placed by governments (*e.g.* the Congo), but mostly it was coordinated with the commercial activities of one or more very large international companies. International public relations firms were frequently hired to execute the programs.

"Country image" advertising, usually in the form of special sections in major national publications of the developed world, designed to promote trade and tourism as well as the significance of the advertiser country. These special sections of paid advertising, sometimes presented in the form of supplements with textual material presented as articles, date back to the period between the two World Wars.

Recently, two changes have occurred. First, the governments of the developing countries have taken complete control of the public relations campaigns formerly supported by foreign corporations. Second, these governments are sponsoring more and more active advocacy and "platform of fact" types of advertising to promote internationally their socio-economic objectives.

Does advertising of this nature—nationally sponsored, and crossing borders to reach audiences in other countries—correspond to the concept of controversy advertising? Apparently it does. The people of the advertiser country are not willing to leave the issues to private diplomatic discussion. The media abroad are perceived as not providing fair, accurate, or complete coverage of the advertiser country's point of view, and use of advertising to state the case affords control over both the message delivered and the environment in which it is communicated.

Is the parallel sustained in the way in which countries and international groupings *use* such advertising? This may be open to debate. For example, Venezuela's President Andres Perez's advertisement advocating nationalization of U.S. oil companies appeared to be an ultimatum to the U.S., just as the later publication of the manifesto of Venezuelan terrorists in North American and European newspapers appeared to be a combined manifesto and ultimatum. We have established earlier the conviction of top corporation executives that they are directly confronting their adversaries in this kind of advertising.

Is there direct confrontation in government-sponsored border-crossing advertisements? Careful inspection of the examples gathered for this survey support these conclusions: (a) The primary targets for this kind of campaign are the people who already agree. This audience is twofold: supporters in the foreign country or countries, and the people at home, who regard this advertising as their voice abroad. (b) The secondary targets are people not clearly committed but who generally fall into the same grouping as the supporters.

The border-crossing advertising by the Third World until recently displayed relatively little sophistication, similar to the "immediate-reaction" and "one-time reply" advertising described in the chapter on "Alternative Message Patterns." This may have reflected on the part of socialist-oriented countries disdain for professional advertising assistance from the developed countries (for example, advertising by some Arab countries, reported to have been financed by multinational oil companies, but presented in a naive format). However, the quality of the advertisements, both in text and graphics, has been improving, suggesting that the real problem has been inexperience and the need to find trustworthy technical assistance. (Such assistance has been abundantly forthcoming—nearly 1,000 advertising and public relations firms are reported by *Business Week* to have approached the Arab oil-producing countries with offers to mount "platform-of-fact" campaigns to present the Arab point of view to the developed countries.)

This use of advertising by nations to present social and economic viewpoints and policies poses the same kinds of questions as those concerning the actions of multinational corporations.

Is there an issue of national sovereignty in use of controversy advertising across borders? Does a national government, or a para-governmental body, have the right to enter and speak directly to the various publics of another country? Without being invited, and solely because it possesses the money to do so?

The issue is minor, of course, so long as the volume of advertising is small. But the amounts of money available to some of the more affluent countries are substantial. It is possible that they could exert strong influence on public opinion and indirect influence on the news content of print media in other countries. Another possibility, though not under existing national and international regulations, is extension of electronic media coverage already discussed. Third World countries might use radio transmission and direct satellite television transmission to developed countries. Both prospects seem unlikely, and would in practice blur the distinction between commercially-controlled advertising and national propaganda. They are nonetheless theoretical possibilities implicit in present trends.

Questions will arise, if the trends continue, about the task of establishing standards and constraints: whether they should be applied by private-enterprise associations, individual national governments, or through some kind of international code, protocol, or administration.

Significant national differences

Controversy advertising does *not* appear in the countries (a) where the media are thought to provide fair coverage of controversial issues, *i.e.* are not viewed as adversary, and (b) where corporate society feels that it has adequate ways of cooperating with government or other bodies of influence, without having to marshall the loyalties of its constituents publicly. It is worth noting that these are countries, such as the Netherlands and Sweden, in which public controversy is not encouraged in general—

even though they are known to possess long-standing traditions of tolerating dissidence. Effort is apparently made to include the dissidents within a kind of consensus-making process. (The alternative is to exclude them totally, tacitly blocking them from funds and access to the media; the dissidents sometimes unconsciously cooperate by refusing to participate.)

It would appear that controversy advertising is less likely to be found in countries where social and economic priorities are ordered through very strong governmental mechanisms—sometimes described as "welfare state" provisions. Sides in the decision-making are not taken publicly. Instead, when agreement on policy has been reached, the consensus is announced in a kind of communications program—governmentally or paragovernmentally sponsored—which strongly resembles a broad newproduct introduction.

This hypothesis is confirmed by the fact that such consensus-type policy announcements, if handled through advertising at all, are presented as public-service campaigns, using the broadest possible audience as a target, rather than the more narrowly defined constituencies of controversy campaigns.

Some spokesmen for the countries displaying this pattern argue that it is a more economical procedure. They maintain that advertising funds for debate of economic and social points of view are not available (certainly true in some economies) and that even in the wealthiest countries, such debate in advertising columns is at best not dignified, and at worst, economically wasteful. This position amounts to a socio-economic variation on the classical argument that advertising simply adds to the cost of doing business—in this case the business of socio-economic decision-making. Corporate proponents of this argument are thus taking a position elsewhere associated with adversary or counter-culture groups.

Conversely, it is interesting to find that adversaries in some of these countries are seeking to employ advertising to democratize the decisionmaking process. They thus gain access to public opinion which they feel they have otherwise been denied.

Opposition to the use of controversy advertising

Even within countries such as the U.S. and U.K. there is strong disagreement about the value of controversy advertising. John O'Toole states one side when he argues:

> You not only have the right to express your point of view, but as a company whose product, pricing, and activities affect many people, you have an obligation to let your customers know where you stand on issues that affect you and them jointly.

His dismay at resistance to this position, even from the people he expects to support him, is reflected in his comment that

> I'm bewildered as to why some of you, whose income as well as rights may be affected by all this, aren't making as much noise as I.

He answers his own bewilderment elsewhere, when he comments that

> Many companies feel that their products should maintain separate and unrelated dialogues with consumers, and . . . a corporate identity should only be evident to share-holders, if at all.

There is a very clear schism in the business community between those firms which choose to speak out ("high profile") and those which feel such speaking out is at best embarrassing, at worse subversive ("low profile"). There is a further concealed schism between those who generally speak out and those who profess to speak out but are not altogether frank.

The advertising director of one of the world's most important newspapers, in terms of its political and economic influence, stated during an interview that he is "opposed to corporate advertising entirely. You properly explain your company through your products. . . ."

Dr. Treasure of J. Walter Thompson stated this position in the most neutral manner possible at the corporate communications seminar in Amsterdam:

> I think there is a great deal to be said in favor of businessmen concentrating on their jobs as businessmen, and leaving the major issues of social progress to be prosecuted by government through its legislation and fiscal policies . . . Despite all the frothy fashionable talk, I think that is eventually what will happen in most cases.

In fact, the issue is one of access to decision-making at the national level. Use of controversy advertising is a way of demanding access to the policy process, by appealing to and marshalling a broader, more democratic constituency. The traditional position of leaving government to the governors begs the question of who is to do the governing, and denies participation of advocate and adversary alike.

11

Problems for the Future

THE ADVERTISING industry of the world welcomes controversy advertising as a new source of income and growth, and as a new kind of challenge to its communications skills. The industry is caught, however, between the sectors of business which regard such expenditure as waste, or as opening up a Pandora's box of issues to unconstructive criticism, and the critics who see advertising as a cynical manipulation of communications for profit, without regard to moral values or social and economic impact.

Controversy becomes the fashion

While still resisted in some countries, controversy advertising appears to have become the fashionable "thing to do" among U.S. advertisers in certain industries.

Involvement in controversy appears to have become a desirable characteristic of corporate image, at least in the eyes of some advertisers. The evolution of a recent Pennwalt advertisement in the U.S. seems to illustrate this point. The original advertisement presented a simple fable about productivity and earnings, in which Pennwalt was advocating private enterprise as against income support for the economically non-productive. This is, of course, a basic economic controversy in many countries. Almost immediately thereafter, Pennwalt produced advertisements incorporating the fable into a larger context, juxtaposing the company's point of view with its activities and earnings record. The fable was apparently not intended to play a role in the controversy, but to describe the corporation to an audience of stockholders and potential investors, and to the financial community at large.

Indiscriminate inclusion of controversial issues in all manner of advertisements, whether done naively or with an exploitative purpose, may give all controversy advertising a bad name. Audiences exposed to such advertisements may soon come to regard them as "all alike" and discount their content. Adversaries will point to the lack of sincerity of the exploitative advertisements and find justification for condemning those which present a genuine point of view. This seems to be an immediate problem in the U.S., and to a lesser extent in the U.K. It is a potential problem in all countries where the levels of per capita or of corporate advertising expenditure are substantial.

Advertising "mass" and fairness

All the critics and opponents of controversy advertising express the same fear: that massive employment of advertising to communicate a point of view can "swamp" and "drown" alternative points of view. This is regarded as undemocratic bullying, contrary to the spirit of fair play in public debate.

The fear of massive sums being moved around to take sides in a controversy is not limited to the adversaries of business. In fact, the only complaints registered by the U.K. Advertising Standards Authority about the Government's anti-inflation advertising came from competitors of businessmen pictured and quoted in the campaign. They felt that the Government advertisements would give these businessmen an unfair advantage. In the same way, smaller companies in the petroleum and other energy-related businesses have been known to complain privately about the large expenditures of Mobil Oil Corporation, American Electric Power, and others during the energy crisis.

The "fairness" issue in the U.S. is unique and, especially as it concerns access to broadcast media, too complex to be explored in depth in this report. It is worth noting, however, that one of the arguments against permitting Mobil access to television for its energy messages was "massive expenditures." As noted several times in the preceding text, Mobil responded by offering to match each minute of its television time with funds for an opponent to present a minute of reply. That the offer was not accepted had little to do with the complexities it posed, such as determining to which Mobil advertisements there should be a response, and who should make it. Mobil's adversaries would have leapt at the chance for such free time. The real opposition came from large corporations, including other energy companies, which did not wish to become involved in controversy advertising for reasons of policy or expense. (More recently, the U.S. energy companies have displayed less resistance to controversy advertising than was previously the case.)

Adversary critics, attacking the allegedly massive expenditures for corporate advertising in the U.S. have tried to drive up the cost of doing it by attacking its tax status. They take the position that it is "grass-roots lobbying," which is not deductible as a business expense under U.S. tax laws.

On this score, there is some conflict within the business community. Most U.S. corporations believe that the purpose of controversy advertising is to protect their good will and interests, and hence tax-deductible. Mobil has taken the position, however, that while most of its corporate advertising is properly tax-deductible, about a quarter of it, which actively urges economic and social policies, is hence of a political cast and subject to tax.

Controversy advertising appears to be most feared as potentially "unfair" on the grounds that only very large corporations can afford to spend massive amounts on it. Is this fear justified? Are there any examples where massive expenditures have given a large corporate advertiser an impact which unfairly dwarfed opposing views?

The research for this study has discovered no examples where advertising *mass* has been a deterrent to publicizing other points of view. A major finding, already presented, is that most controversy advertising talks to its supporters and potential supporters. Too heavy a barrage might easily be counter-productive in its impact on this audience, causing fatigue, boredom, irritation, and even re-examination of their support.

The great bulk of advertising involved in any controversy is focused on clarification of the facts. This "platform-of-fact" advertising excites no fear and little criticism, so long as its content is truthful. People are fearful and resentful only of overt policy-pleading, ultimatums, and manifestos. While such advertising is conspicuous, it constitutes not more than 5% of controversy advertising in the U.S. and probably less than that in other countries.

The big corporations feel that adversaries and smaller companies have access to media, through news coverage, which they cannot obtain at any price, that this coverage is often unfair to large companies, and that their expenditure of large sums is therefore justified. Three theoretical positions support the large corporation's argument that it has a *right* to spend money for advertising in order to have a voice in public controversy.

First is that the company is an aggregate of individuals who own it. These individuals have the right to join collectively in advocating policies which will benefit them. Second is that the company is an aggregate also of the individuals who work for it and who also merit a collective voice. And third is that the company has the right to support policies which will ensure continuing and improved service to its loyal customers.

These three arguments applied to a *small* firm are generally accepted. It is only in relation to the very large firm that they suddenly appear suspect in the public mind. On close inspection, it appears that the real fear is of the potential ability of the large corporation to use communications in a massive way to *mislead* and to dominate audience's minds with distortions and un-truths, so that the opposition has no way to set the facts straight. It is the "Big Lie" that is feared.

Fairness, media access, and communications skill

Two reasons are commonly given for the fear of the "Big Lie" in controversy advertising. First, it is argued that the major media are accessible only to advertisers with large amounts of money to spend. In fact, this is only true for television and, as a matter of policy, no country in the world currently permits large corporations to advertise explicit economic and social points of view in the broadcast media. The much lower costs of advertising in print media make it possible for an advertiser to use them at almost any level of expenditure.

Second, it is argued that only advertisers with large amounts of money to spend can command the talents of the most skilled creators of advertising, the large, renowned agencies and the specialists who demand high fees. The facts do not support this argument. Many of the examples in this book show that excellent and effective controversy advertising has been produced by all sizes of advertising agencies, as well as small groups of consultants and even (in the Case Examples of "Rats" and "I Want Out") by volunteers working outside any formal structure. The amounts of money available to large corporations do not, therefore, appear to give them an unfair advantage over other advertisers in access to superior advertising skills.

Problems of verification

The issue of verifying the information content rarely arises in controversy advertising campaigns that are continuous, expertly planned, and presented with professional skill. Just as these "platform of fact" campaigns are generally acceptable to broadcast media, so the factual explanations they so dramatically communicate are generally praised by journalists and are greeted with silence by adversaries and with envy by competitors. Accusations of unfairness in controversy advertising are made almost entirely in connection with defensive and aggressive postures. This advertising usually involves immediate or very rapid reply, with a minimum number of approval levels and controls, and direct involvement of top management.

Empirically classified, four different categories of unfairness appear in controversy advertising:

1. *Misstatement of facts.*
2. *Selective use of facts to mislead.* Only the supporting facts are presented. In cases where these are clearly outweighed by negative points, the argument is deemed misleading and unfair.
3. *Fallacious arguments.* The advertiser is accused of spending money to present an argument which cannot be defended. For example, a large U.S. bank has taken a position in a major campaign which many economists say cannot be defended.
4. *Use of visual, audio, and/or graphic devices to* influence the audience emotionally in favor of the advertiser's argument for non-rational reasons.

Adversaries of large corporations and critics of controversy advertising contend that there are many examples of all four categories of unfairness. Others observe that misstatements of fact are more commonly found in the advertising of small firms than large, and more in product advertising than in advertising about points of view. Selective use of facts is prevalent, but statements made by large corporations are immediately subject to scrutiny not only by adversary media, but also by competitors and by the financial community. Few companies of any size are willing to risk criticism from these audiences.

The accusation of "fallacious arguments" is more difficult to document. The question centers on whether or not an argument is acceptable in the context of the controversies of the day. Is American Electric Power justified in advocating greater coal production? Are the Mobil and Allied Chemical arguments for corporate profits reasonable? The adversary position is that large corporations have no right to spend *so much money* advertising their points of view, *if their points of view are wrong.* But who is to be arbiter of the truth?

Accusations of unfairness are also made against techniques which, intentionally or not, evoke emotional responses which are strongly resented by people who dislike influences of this kind. Nonetheless, the adversary users of controversy advertising appear to be just as adept as large corporations, perhaps even more so, in using dramatic illustrations, effective color, persuasive sound, memorable slogans to give their messages impact. The "I Want Out" poster is a good case in point.

Problems of regulation

The issue of substantiating truth and upholding fairness in controversy advertising has been effectively avoided by both the statutory and self-regulatory bodies that oversee advertising in most countries. As already seen, the broadcast industry worldwide, with or without government approval, has generally chosen to prevent business from using those media to argue its cases. Advertising industry organizations such as the National Advertising Review Board in the U.S., the Advertising Standards Authority in the U.K., and others have adopted no procedures to examine social and economic points of view presented in privately sponsored advertising. In some countries, the force of business opinion tends to suppress such advertising entirely.

The issue of government regulation of fairness is being debated in several countries now. Two courses are advocated. The first is to give wide-reaching powers to government regulatory bodies, such as the U.S. Federal Trade Commission, the U.K. Office of Fair Trading, and the ombudsmen in other countries, to intervene in controversy advertising. This idea is a matter of great concern, since it is viewed by many legal authorities as conflicting directly with traditions and laws ensuring freedom of speech and opinion.

A second course, intended to ensure freedom of expression to the advertiser, but also to provide a "balanced" opportunity for adversary reply, involves extending the proposal made by Mobil Oil Corporation to all controversy advertising that advocates public policy: if a company should run 25,000 monetary units of advertising to defend its profit position, its adversaries would be provided equivalent advertising space or time to state an opposing case. The proposal seems naive. How would the respondent be selected? As we have already seen, most controversy situations do not divide into a neat dichotomy of advocate and adversary.

Controversy advertising by business is subject to very careful scrutiny by several groups. Questions of factual error and omission are analyzed by the press and regulated by a wide variety of business and government bodies. Fallacious arguments are subject to a different kind of regulation: the ridicule of one's peers. The use of emotional persuasion is available to all. Such skills have always served to render equal the Davids with the Goliaths.

In fact, judging from the research for this volume, unfair and misleading information is more often found in business or government sponsored public-service advertising, approved by public consensus and subject to no regulation, than it is in controversy advertising. Attacks on the fairness of controversy advertising will doubtless continue to be the most significant issue, and they will involve not simply the large corporations—

Big Business—but also government bodies (Big Government), politicians, socioeconomic and even religious movements, and, as border-crossing gains in significance, affluent countries as well.

In the many examples studied, abuse of truth and fairness has been much more characteristic of small companies, associations, *ad hoc* "action committees," and adversary political units, all with comparatively limited funds for advertising—rather than of the large companies. The underlying reasons for fear of corporate size are profound, however, and not likely to be argued away on a rational basis.

12

The Future?

THE HISTORICAL view of controversy advertising suggests that it is a product of periods of economic expansion. The spread of affluence in such periods encourages new publics to expect or demand a voice in social and economic decision-making. Discussion has moved over the years into the public media, where controversy receives wide coverage, with new adversary points of view commanding the most attention.

The new voices experiment with new media and with new uses of conventional media, advertising being an important means of communication. In the ensuing debate, the advocates of established socioeconomic structures have had recourse to paid controversy advertising to restore the balance upset in news coverage and to fight for competition position. Recent economic reverses and social turbulence have raised the pitch of controversy advertising abruptly.

In *every* country of the world where advertising expenditures are a significant force in the economy, the controversy advertising developed in the U.S. and U.K. has contributed to three kinds of developments (see Case Examples):

1. Increased volume of corporate advertising to explain products and services, to respond to controversy that has grown internationally.
2. Evidence of social awareness introduced into advertising programs, either in the texts and subjects chosen for product advertising, or in separate controversy campaigns to state overall corporate viewpoints.

3. Greatly increased emphasis on specific detail and facts. (Comparative advertising, where it is permitted or accepted, may owe its new strength to the effort to present the "full competitive picture" in as straightforward a manner as possible.)

Corporate advertising has been permanently altered by the outspoken controversy campaigns by major U.S. and U.K. advertisers, even if large advertisers in other countries are only gradually following suit. The vague, benevolent postures of corporate giants attacked by Tom Wicker and Irving Kristol are no longer acceptable for corporate image campaigns. Attempts to substitute broad statements of economic philosophy and prestigious nonverbal presentations of art and culture have already been scrutinized for their sincerity. The alternatives appear to be (a) clear statements of corporate position, in a manner open to public discussion and verification, or (b) (as some recommend) no statements at all. But a non-profile is not realistic because it leaves the field to adversaries in the media and to competitors.

Heightened social awareness that has developed in nearly every country, proliferation of special interests, segmentation within society, media that are responsive to social change—all guarantee that controversy advertising is not a passing phenomenon. The issues raised in this study will therefore remain relevant, however much their locus may shift to different sectors of society and economy, to new media, and to new parts of the world.

Case Examples

NOTE: The following case examples have been selected to illustrate and support the ideas presented in the analytical text. They are not presented as a representative cross-section of what is happening in controversy advertising worldwide, nor has the attempt been made to include all the campaigns exciting the most controversy.

The texts of the case examples were drafted on the basis of research and interviews, and then submitted to the advertisers for their revision and approval. In some cases, the revision was extensive. The texts, as they appear here, are published in the exact wording approved by each advertiser.

Cadillac Motor Car Company

1915, 1929

Objective: Originally, to present the case for
high standards in manufacturing quality,
in connection with a specific product question.

Thereafter, presented as a basic statement
of business philosophy of relevance during
difficult times. A justification of
the "free enterprise" system and its
contribution even under conditions of attack.

Execution: Single advertisement, prepared by the Cadillac
advertising agency (MacManus Inc., known today
as D'Arcy-MacManus & Masius) at the client's
request. Written by Theodore F. MacManus
himself, in terms of the client's brief.

Media: A single insertion in The Saturday Evening Post
(national weekly consumer magazine), January 2,
1915.

Reprints for sales promotion purposes, as a result
of requests (continuing to this day).

National newspaper campaign, mid-February 1929.

Results: No formal measurement, but the immediate
demand for reprints from 1915 on is a clear
indication of strong interest in this advertisement's
message. Considered one of the great classics
of American advertising, and cited in Julian
Watkins' book, The One Hundred Great Advertisements
(U.S.).

Advertisement reproduction Courtesy of Cadillac Division,
General Motors Company.

The

PENALTY OF LEADERSHIP

IN every field of human endeavor, he that is first must perpetually live in the white light of publicity. ¶Whether the leadership be vested in a man or in a manufactured product, emulation and envy are ever at work. ¶In art, in literature, in music, in industry, the reward and the punishment are always the same. ¶The reward is widespread recognition; the punishment, fierce denial and detraction. ¶When a man's work becomes a standard for the whole world, it also becomes a target for the shafts of the envious few. ¶If his work be merely mediocre, he will be left severely alone—if he achieve a masterpiece, it will set a million tongues a-wagging. ¶Jealousy does not protrude its forked tongue at the artist who produces a commonplace painting. ¶Whatsoever you write, or paint, or play, or sing, or build, no one will strive to surpass, or to slander you, unless your work be stamped with the seal of genius. ¶Long, long after a great work or a good work has been done, those who are disappointed or envious continue to cry out that it can not be done. ¶Spiteful little voices in the domain of art were raised against our own Whistler as a mountebank, long after the big world had acclaimed him its greatest artistic genius. ¶Multitudes flocked to Bayreuth to worship at the musical shrine of Wagner, while the little group of those whom he had dethroned and displaced argued angrily that he was no musician at all. ¶The little world continued to protest that Fulton could never build a steamboat, while the big world flocked to the river banks to see his boat steam by. ¶The leader is assailed because he is a leader, and the effort to equal him is merely added proof of that leadership. ¶Failing to equal or to excel, the follower seeks to depreciate and to destroy—but only confirms once more the superiority of that which he strives to supplant. ¶There is nothing new in this. ¶It is as old as the world and as old as the human passions—envy, fear, greed, ambition, and the desire to surpass. ¶And it all avails nothing. ¶If the leader truly leads, he remains—the leader. ¶Master-poet, master-painter, master-workman, each in his turn is assailed, and each holds his laurels through the ages. ¶That which is good or great makes itself known, no matter how loud the clamor of denial. ¶That which deserves to live—lives.

The Warner & Swasey Co.

1936 to present, continuing

Objective: To sell Warner & Swasey products to top
management through stating the case for the
contribution which business makes to the
U.S. economy.

Execution: Conceived by Warner & Swasey top management
and written as a series, principally by a single
copywriter, Kenneth Akers, of the Griswold-
Eshleman Company agency, Cleveland. Copywriter
writes to subjects suggested by management, or
submits suggestions of his own. Advertisements
are approved at top management level.

Media: Business publications (Business Week, Forbes,
The Wall Street Journal, Industry Week) and
newsmagazines with a business orientation
(Time, Newsweek, U.S. News & World Report).
Schedule has been consistent over years, with
regular frequency and special position in
magazines.

Results: Strong acceptance in the business community,
with requests for reprints. Strong press
comment (ncluding radio and TV).

                  Syndicated readership services consistently report
high readership scores, outstanding scores for
certain advertisements.

                  Demand for reprints is so strong that the company
has published a selection of them as a 92-page
booklet, which is now in its 12th edition.

                  The advertisement shown ("Wonder what a Frenchman
thinks about") is cited in Watkins' book,
The One Hundred Greatest Advertisements (U.S.).
At the time the advertisement appeared, in
September 1941, about five million requests for
reprints were received by the company.

Advertisement reproduction Courtesy of The Warner & Swasey
Company.

Wonder what a Frenchman thinks about

Two years ago a Frenchman was as free as you are. Today what does he think—

—as he humbly steps into the gutter to let his conquerors swagger past,

—as he works 53 hours a week for 30 hours' pay,

—as he sees all trade unions outlawed and all the "rights" for which he sacrificed his country trampled by his foreign masters,

—as he sees his wife go hungry and his children face a lifetime of serfdom.

What does that Frenchman—soldier, workman, politician or business man—think today? Probably it's something like this—"I wish I had been less greedy for myself and more anxious for my country; I wish I had realized you can't beat off a determined invader by a quarreling, disunited people at home; I wish I had been willing to give in on some of my rights to other Frenchmen instead of giving up all of them to a foreigner; I wish I had realized other Frenchmen had rights, too; I wish I had known that patriotism is *work*, not talk, *giving*, not getting."

And if that Frenchman could read our newspapers today, showing pressure groups each demanding things be done for them instead of for our country, wouldn't he say to American business men, politicians, soldiers and workmen—"If you knew the horrible penalty your action is bound to bring, you'd bury your differences now before they bury you; you'd work for your country as you never worked before, and wait for your private ambitions until your country is safe. Look at me . . . I worked too little and too late."

**WARNER
&
SWASEY**
Turret Lathes
Cleveland

103

Chesapeake & Ohio Railway - Nickel Plate Road

Late 1945 - mid-1946

Objective: To dramatize the situation in rail transport
in the U.S., and to further merger among
rail lines in such a way as to improve
passenger service.

The advertisement specifically questions
a situation whereby human passengers were
required to change trains on trans-continental
trips, while merchandise could be moved
coast to coast without trans-shipping.

Organization
structure: This single advertisement was inserted
into a continuing commercial campaign for
the Chesapeake & Ohio Railway. The subject
was generated by a remark made by Robert
R. Young, Chairman of the railroad advertising,
and turned into an advertisement by the
creative team assigned to the C&O account
at the Kenyon & Eckhardt advertising agency.

Because of the sensitivity of the account,
the advertising campaign was at the time handled
through direct contact between the copy chief
of the agency and the railroad's chairman.
The advertisement was written and set in type
with a layout in a single day, and approved
directly by Mr. Young (by telephone) the
following morning.

Media: The "hog ad" was used initially as a subject
in an on-going campaign in Time Magazine and
daily newspapers in major cities. Reprints
were also mailed to prominent businessmen.

Results: High noting scores in Time. Widespread
comment in the press and on the radio.
The advertisement is considered a classic in
American advertising.

The specific objective of the advertisement
was never achieved, however, and the problems
raised by Mr. Young in this and other
activities were never resolved.

A Hog Can Cross the Country Without Changing Trains—But YOU Can't!

The Chesapeake & Ohio Railway and the Nickel Plate Road are again proposing to give human beings a break!

It's hard to believe, but it's true.

If you want to ship a hog from coast to coast, he can make the entire trip without changing cars. You can't. It is impossible for you to pass through Chicago, St. Louis, or New Orleans without breaking your trip!

There is an invisible barrier down the middle of the United States which you cannot cross without inconvenience, lost time, and trouble.

560,000 Victims in 1945!

If you want to board a sleeper on one coast and ride through to the other, you must make double Pullman reservations, pack and transfer your baggage, often change stations, and wait around for connections.

It's the same sad story if you make a relatively short trip. You can't cross that mysterious line! To go from Fort Wayne to Milwaukee or from Cleveland to Des Moines, you must also stop and change trains.

Last year alone, more than 560,000 people were forced to make annoying, time-wasting stopovers at the phantom Chinese wall which splits America in half!

End the Secrecy!

Why should travel be less convenient for people than it is for pigs? Why should Americans be denied the benefits of through train service? No one has yet been able to explain it.

Canada has this service . . . with a choice of two routes. Canada isn't split down the middle. Why should we be? No reasonable answer has yet been given. Passengers still have to stop off at Chicago, St. Louis, and New Orleans—although they can ride right through other important rail centers.

It's time to pry the lid off this mystery. It's time for action to end this inconvenience to the travelling public . . . NOW!

Many railroads could cooperate to provide this needed through service. To date, the Chesapeake & Ohio and the Nickel Plate ALONE have made a public offer to do so.

How about it !

Once more we would like to go on record with this specific proposal:

The Chesapeake & Ohio, whose western passenger terminus is Cincinnati, stands ready now to join with any combination of other railroads to set up connecting transcontinental and intermediate service through Chicago and St. Louis, on practical schedules and routes.

The Nickel Plate Road, which runs to Chicago and St. Louis, also stands ready now to join with any combination of roads to set up the same kind of connecting service through these two cities.

Through railroad service can't be blocked forever. The public wants it. It's bound to come. Again, we invite the support of the public, of railroad people and railroad investors—for this vitally needed improvement in rail transportation!

Chesapeake & Ohio Railway · Nickel Plate Road

Terminal Tower, Cleveland 1, Ohio

105

Ohio Consolidated Telephone Company

1956

Objective: To alert the local community to the serious
               consequences of vandalistic tactics against
               a telephone company, during a strike

Execution: A series of advertisements was prepared by
               a task force, working out of a motel in the
               strike area. The team consisted of a copywriter,
               the public relations director of the parent
               company for the area (General Telephone Company),
               plus support services from the agency's head-
               quarters. Agency was Howard Swink Advertising,
               Marion, Ohio. Copy was prepared on a short-term
               basis, without testing, and approved directly
               (in person or by telephone) by the regional
               public relations director and the president of
               the company.

Media: Local newspaper (full pages) and local radio
               (15-second spots).

Results: Vandalism on the part of unidentified supporters
               of the telephone workers' union was reduced
               during the period of negotiations, easing
               communications between the company and the union.
               The strike was resolved on an amicable basis.

The Case of

THE
AMPUTATED
TELEPHONE

You'd fight if somebody attacked your house with an axe, wouldn't you?

What about the vital lifeline between your home and your doctor . . . between your home and police protection . . . between your home and your far away loved ones . . . *your telephone?*

Recently, in your town, or in towns near you—this vital link *has been attacked*. Telephone service has been interrupted, interfered with, or entirely cut off!

Where? In Cadiz, in Portsmouth, New Boston, Circleville, Cambridge, St. Marys . . .

Since July 15, when the strike against Ohio Consolidated began, more than 50 cables have been cut, slashed, burned, hacked in half—interfering with the phone service of more than SIX THOUSAND homes and businesses!

Supervisors manning local and long distance telephone boards—trying desperately to keep the lines open to *you*—have been harassed, threatened, intimidated, even shot at!

More than ten offices have had to be closed down for short or long periods—due to vandalism or because police protection was not adequate to handle the danger to operators and equipment!

Our Pledge

We pledge that we will do our utmost to see that your telephone service is NOT interrupted. We are constantly running service level checks to find out what kind of service you are receiving. Supervisors are working long overtime hours manning the boards, repairing the damaged equipment —far beyond the call of duty. They will go on fighting—for YOU.

We pledge, furthermore, that we will not ask you to pay for service you have not received. We will adjust your bills, and charge you only the amount which we can fairly ask.

We pledge these things—as part of the public trust we serve—and we will do them.

But one thing we cannot do—we cannot guarantee that you will have phone service when you need it most. Someone with an axe may chop into your line—or terrify a girl into leaving her telephone board. We will do our best to give you service again—as fast as we can. But who will stop the man who cut you off?

OHIO CONSOLIDATED TELEPHONE COMPANY

"Rats"
Volunteer group
(Bert Steinhauser and Chuck Kollewe)

September, 1967

Objective:
To produce public pressure sufficient to reverse a vote in the U.S. House of Representatives, which had defeated the "Rat Extermination" bill.

Execution:
Two Doyle Dane Bernbach creative men, out of indignation over the initial defeat of the rat-extermination bill, set up their own _ad_ _hoc_ organization to shift the voting balance in the House of Representatives through advertising.

Advertisement was created by Steinhauser and Kollewe and assembled at minimum cost. Placement was direct with publications.

Media:
Single advertisement appeared twice, once in New York Review of Books (high-level intellectual publication), and once in local weekly newspaper, Pelham, N.Y. Sun.

Continuing campaign had been planned, but results of initial advertisement made this effort unnecessary.

Results:
Upon publication, the advertisement drew instant nation-wide attention. It was shown on television, read on radio, and reproduced as news in newspapers and magazines.

The rat-extermination bill was immediately re-presented in the House of Representatives and was passed, providing significant funding for rat-control in U.S. urban slums.

The creators of the advertisement received a personal letter of commendation from the President of the United States.

NOTE: This case does not qualify for the subject of this book, in the sense that the two insertions were published at no cost by the media. In every other sense, however, it was an example of advertising professionalism applied to a situation of controversy.

Advertisement reproduction Courtesy of Bert Steinhauser and Chuck Kollewe.

Cut this out and put it in bed next to your child.

Go ahead. Try it, if you have the stomach for it. Lay it next to your baby and let him play with it.

You can't?

Then you have a lot more imagination than some of the members of our House of Representatives.

They don't even think real rats are anything to worry about.

That's why they laughed when they killed a bill that would have given $40 million to our cities and states to help them pay for rat-control programs in our slums.

But the real shame is that they didn't even vote on the bill itself. They only voted on a rule that asked them to consider it.

And they voted 207 to 176 against it.

They had their reasons, of course. Economy was the most quoted one. They felt this country couldn't afford $40 million.

Yet they were told that rats cause us an estimated $900 million worth of damage each year.

Does that make economic sense?

They were also told that rats have killed more humans than all the generals in history put together. And that thousands of our children are bitten by rats each year—some killed or disfigured.

Does that make social sense? Especially when we're already spending Federal money to protect livestock and grains from rats?

Maybe those men have never lived in broken-down tenements where you could hear the rats scurrying inside the walls at night.

Maybe they've never seen a rat dash across their kitchen floor and into some hole under the sink when a light was snapped on.

Maybe. But then a lot of us have been that lucky. Does that excuse our ignoring those who haven't?

There are 90 million rats in this country. Where do you think they go when their slum homes are torn down?

They go into our finest hotels and restaurants; into modern apartment buildings, cellars, garages. They go everywhere and anywhere.

And they breed more rats.

That's why when our congressmen vote against getting rid of rats, they're voting against all of us. Not just the poor people. But all of us.

Fortunately, there's still hope.

The vote was 207 to 176. That means if we can get just 16 men to change their votes when the bill comes up again, the tally will be 192 to 191—enough to pass it.

Below is a list of congressmen and how they voted.

If yours voted for the bill, write him and let him know you support him and anything he can do to change the minds of those who voted against it.

If yours voted against the bill, write and let him know you want him to change his vote.

Write to: Honorable _____
House of Representatives, Washington, D. C.

It's time we stopped giving rats equal rights with people.

FOR THE RAT EXTERMINATION BILL—176				AGAINST THE RAT EXTERMINATION BILL—207			

A message from some citizens who think **Congress made a mistake.**

109

Volunteer group
(I Want Out, Inc.)

1969-1970

Objective: "Un-sell the war in South Viet Nam."
                (Turn American public opinion against support
                of U.S.-led hostilities against the insurgent
                forces in the nation of Viet Nam.)

Execution: An ad hoc "advertising agency" formed by
                professionals on a volunteer basis, and led
                by David McCall, Chairman of the Board of the
                McCaffrey & McCall advertising agency, New York.
                Advertisements were developed in a conventional
                agency and submitted to a "Blue Ribbon" committee
                of communications and government experts for
                approval. Advertisements were prepared in a
                short time-frame and published without testing.

Media: Principally television and radio, especially
                in southern and southwest U.S. Poster (shown
                as illustration of case) gained widespread
                acceptance and was sold as a money-raiser for
                activity.

Results: Campaign received widespread recognition, but
                also encountered considerable resistance from
                media, particularly newspapers. The ad hoc
                organization faded and materials were passed to
                the U.S. National Council of Churches, which
                continued the effort. The extent to which the
                campaign contributed to the eventual withdrawal
                of the U.S. from Viet Nam (197) cannot be
                measured.

NOTE: This case does not qualify for the subject of this book,
in the sense that the advertisements were accepted without
payment by the media which used them. In every other sense,
however, the case is an example of advertising professionalism
outside of the conventional structure of public-service advertising.

Mobil Oil Corporation

1971 to present, continuing

Objective: To present the Mobil point of view on a variety of issues concerning the company and the country.

Execution: The campaign was initiated in 1971 by Mobil, working with the company's long-term advertising agency, Doyle Dane Bernbach. Since 1973, Mobil's public affairs advertising has been prepared by the company's Public Affairs Department, which functions as a de facto creative unit. The agency contributes ideas and suggestions, and provides all other agency functions, including definition of target audiences (demographics), monitoring of syndicated research services, etc.

The steady evolution of creative approach -- from a strongly militant stance during the energy/economic crisis to a variety of approaches in 1976 -- has been internally generated.

Mobil's public affairs advertising is prepared in conjunction with an elaborate program of sponsorship of television series, both on the U.S. "public" (i.e. non-commercial) networks and stations, where Mobil in fact contributes to the cost of the programing, and also on commercial stations.

Media: The so-called "Op-Ed" campaign (a unique advertising format consisting of a quarter-page advertisement, on the commentary page facing the newspaper's editorial comments, an idea originated by the New York Times), is published on a weekly schedule in daily newspapers of national influence.

The "Observations" column, an editorial-style mix of light-hearted and serious comments on affairs of the day, appears on a weekly basis in "Sunday supplements" -- that is, magazines·included in the Sunday editions of daily newspapers (New York Times Sunday Magazine, Parade, Family Weekly, etc.).

Periodically, the company has used full-page advertisements in key newspapers (New York Times, Washington Post) to express its stand concerning issues of immediacy.

Results: Mobil does not have a systematic program for measuring impact of the public affairs campaign, but "informal" measures indicate strong attention in target audiences.

Mobil advertising activities have received remarkable coverage in the U.S. press, and the public affairs campaign is widely considered as the single most significant campaign of this nature ever undertaken.-- regardless of country. The Chairman of the Mobil Oil Corporation, Mr. Rawleigh Warner, was named "Advertising Man of the Year" by Advertising Age in 1975.

Advertisements reproduction Courtesy of Mobil Oil Corporation.

⊙bservations

A fable for now. "At last, seeing some pebbles lie near the place, he cast them one by one into the pitcher; and thus, by degrees, raised the water up to the very brim, and satisfied his thirst." Thus did Aesop describe the crow's ingenuity in getting water out of a high-necked pitcher. However, that approach isn't strictly for the birds; oil people do about the same thing, but instead of pebbles they inject water, steam, chemicals, carbon dioxide, or gas into sluggish oilfields to recover otherwise unrecoverable oil. If such techniques could coax existing fields to yield an extra 10% of their remaining oil, the result would equal about 33 billion barrels—roughly the amount of America's current proved reserves. That would be worth crowing about.

O

Quiz. There's disagreement over exactly what would happen if the 18 largest oil companies were broken up, as proposed in pending "divestiture" legislation. What do you think would happen?

a. Gasoline and heating oil prices would be likely to go up, not down. (T) (F)
b. Smaller companies would have trouble raising capital to develop domestic energy sources. (T) (F)
c. Smaller companies would be in a weaker bargaining position to shop for foreign oil we have to import. (T) (F)
d. The U.S. would be more vulnerable to a foreign oil embargo or price increases. (T) (F)
e. The effect on the total economy could be severe, leading to a new recession and more unemployment. (T) (F)
f. Congress would then try to break up large companies in other industries. (T) (F)

We're convinced the answers are all "true" and we'll be happy to provide further information if you write us. Not everyone may agree; but since it's impossible to predict the future with certainty, the real question for the nation is whether divestiture is a risk worth running.

O

"GOD WORKS IN MYSTERIOUS WAYS. MY ONLY THOUGHT WHEN I JOINED THIS CAR POOL, MISS WILLIAMS, WAS TO SAVE ENERGY."

O

Follow that cab. To the Museum of Modern Art. That's where "The Taxi Project" will be on exhibit from now to Sept. 7. Made possible by grants from Mobil and the U.S. Urban Mass Transportation Administration, the exhibit features fresh ideas from four American and European automakers. Each cab represents a glimpse of the future. They're safer, more comfortable, more efficient, less polluting, and roomier than today's models. (Even built to accommodate a mother with a baby carriage or a person in a wheelchair.) If the idea starts your meter running—MOMA is at 11 West 53rd Street.

Mobil

Observations, Box A, Mobil Oil Corporation, 150 East 42 Street, New York, N.Y. 10017

© 1976 Mobil Oil Corporation

The soapbox is a lonely place

For a long time now, we've been raising our voice in ads like this one. On a variety of issues. Including the need for a sensible U.S. energy policy. Noting that without adequate return on investment, exploration for new sources of oil and gas will fall off. Making the U.S. more and more dependent on costly foreign supplies.

Sometimes, we wonder if we are talking to ourselves. Congress certainly wasn't listening when it singled out the oil industry for heavy new taxation. In addition, there are now some 500 oil-related bills before Congress, many of which would impose new regulation on the industry. Some Congressmen have even proposed a subsidized federal petroleum corporation to "compete" with private oil companies.

We don't think the companies should be expected to take such assaults lying down. So we speak out. The trouble is, not enough other businesses follow suit—and it gets pretty lonely on the soapbox.

We think there's plenty for other companies to worry about. If our Congressmen can blithely take away the depletion allowance from some oil companies, if they can tinker with the foreign tax credit to "punish" us—and if they do this even at the risk of the nation's future energy security and perhaps the whole economy—what makes anyone think they'll stop with oil?

What makes *any* industry think it's safe?

We wish there were more like the Chase Bank, which has been warning that government disincentives to investment are precipitating a critical shortage of capital. The U.S., says Chase, will need $4.1 trillion in the next ten years, just to rebuild aging industrial capacity.

And if it doesn't happen, there won't be enough jobs. Which suggests other voices should come forth. Not just business, but labor groups. Women. Minorities. Every American who has a stake in the economy. And who doesn't?

If enough voices are raised, Congress will have to listen. And it won't be so lonely out there on the soapbox.

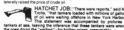
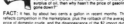

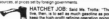
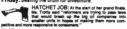

Caterpillar Tractor Co.

1973 to present, and continuing

Objective: To present the "trade-offs" involved in seeking
                solutions to major controversial issues in the U.S.
                today. Long-range solutions inevitably involve
                compromise, falling short of perfection but none-
                theless contributing to the betterment of mankind.
                Products which Caterpillar makes are associated
                with the solutions being sought.

Execution: The present campaign is a continuation of previous
                advertising dating back to 1915, always involved
                with Caterpillar products' social and economic
                contributions. Public awareness studies are used
                to determine Caterpillar's status in the eyes of
                key audiences. In view of the complexity of the
                issues discussed, each advertisement attempts to
                recognize at least two valid viewpoints, then states
                the company's corporate position, with the final line,
                "There are no simple solutions, only intelligent
                choices."

                Because of the nature of the subjects, Caterpillar
                corporate advertisements are initiated and sub-
                stantially written internally, with the direct in-
                volvement of administrative officers.

Media: Newsmagazines, business magazines, general interest
                publications.

Results: Advertisements have obtained good recognition and
                readership with a general audience and the business
                community. Customers for Caterpillar products are
                quite aware of the support these ads provide their
                activities. The copy has been quoted by business
                leaders and reprinted on a voluntary basis by the
                trade press. Readership scores consistently above
                average for industrial advertising.

Advertisement reproduction Courtesy of Caterpillar Tractor Co.

"Coal belongs to the past."

"Coal is our fuel of the future."

Coal. A relic of yesterday? Or our fuel for today and tomorrow? Reason will support either view.

Some people link coal to the past. To a yesterday of smoke-filled air, soot, dirty streams, ashes. The blackened, hollow-eyed faces of miners. Coal, at the century's turn was a dirty fuel. That's one reason why oil and gas took its place. In 1910 coal provided 90% of our energy. Today only 18%.

Many believe our oil and gas will be gone early in the next century. True, they say, there are great reserves. Oil shale. Tar sands. But present extraction methods require huge amounts of capital and tremendous volumes of water. That, plus environmental protection requirements, limit our ability to meet oil needs from these sources. Other energy sources seem equally undeveloped and far away in time. Time may be running out.

What can we do? We need oil and gas. Not only for fuel, but for petrochemicals, pesticides, plastics, rubber products. But the plain fact is our supplies won't last forever.

Fortunately, we do have an alternative fuel: coal. Coal is abundant. Quickly available. And we have the technology to mine and convert it at acceptable economic and environmental cost. And it's versatile. Coal can supply us with chemicals for industry and fuels for transportation. Much the same as oil and gas.

Coal is not only a basic fuel, but it can buy time to develop additional energy sources and do the necessary research to perfect nuclear technology.

Caterpillar products are used in most energy industries. They power drill rigs and pump oil, mine coal and atomic fuels. They reclaim land and prepare power sites. We also share America's concern over availability of ample energy at affordable economic and environmental cost.

There are no simple solutions. Only intelligent choices.

CATERPILLAR

Caterpillar, Cat and ⚙ are Trademarks of Caterpillar Tractor Co.

117

American Electric Power System

Early 1974 through 1975

Objectives: American Electric Power provides electric service
to over 5-3/4 million customers in parts of seven
states. It was deeply concerned about government
decisions and actions in the energy field that it
believed were not based on a reasonable balance of
the large number of competing and sometimes conflicting
public interest considerations. It foresaw an
inadequate and unreliable supply of electric power
in the future to meet the needs of the country,
unless some changes in government policies were made.

The OPEC oil embargo in the fall of 1974 turned a
developing energy supply problem into an energy
crisis. When months passed without the development
of a national energy policy to cope with the crisis,
AEP decided to bring to the attention of the public
and people in government, through a series of advertisements, the severity of the energy crisis and
its potential consequences. It urged, as a fundamental step to solving the crisis, a national energy
policy that would include:

1. A national commitment to coal, America's
   most abundant fossil fuel, in order to conserve
   precious oil and gas for uses where there
   is no substitute.

2. Preservation of the environment through reclamation regulations governing the mining
   of coal in both the Eastern and Western
   U.S.A. fields.

3. Reasonable modification of government regulations that were preventing optimum production
   and use of coal.

4. Rigorous conservation through the efficient
   use of all forms of energy, including all
   fuels and electric power.

In short, a National Energy Policy that would lessen
America's dependence on foreign oil by increasing
America's dependence on coal and conservation, in order
to avert a prolonged shortage of electric power
which would be catastrophic to America's economy.

Execution: The campaign was handled directly by the Chairman of
the Board and chief executive of the Company -- one
of the largest producers of electric power in the
world -- in close association with the company's
Public Affairs department and its advertising agency.

We have more coal than they have oil. Let's use it!

America *is* self-sufficient in one fossil fuel source of energy: COAL. We're sitting on about half of the world's known supply — enough for over 500 years!

It can be the major solution to our present energy problems.

Coal *can* be used instead of oil or gas for the production of electricity.

Electricity, in turn, can be used for virtually all energy needs, except some forms of transportation.

And when electricity is fully put to use, the staggering amounts of oil and gas saved can be diverted to other more critical uses. Such as transportation.

To be sure, burning the coal at hand as well as extracting new coal as quickly as possible, is not without its problems.

And when you start to tick off such things as labor stability, price controls, hopper cars, environmental resistance, new mine de-velopment and land reclamation, the problems seem formidable.

But they are nothing that American ingenuity cannot lick.

Coal — good old reliable coal — can help solve the energy crisis if America is determined to do so, and we have never known timidity to be our national characteristic.

Let's start using that coal. Fully.

Now.

American Electric Power Company, Inc.

119

Advertisements were developed on a week-to-week basis, in order to keep them timely and immediate. They were created by Byrne, Slattery Etal, Inc., an advertising agency long associated with AEP's area development activities. The demand for a high level of creativity throughout the campaign required the personal attention of the agency principals.

In the first year of the campaign, 37 separate advertisements were created in rapid succession, with no more than three ever prepared in advance; frequency of initiation of subjects thereafter slowed somewhat, but maximum flexibility of action was maintained.

Media: Newsweeklies: Time, Newsweek, U.S. News & World Report.
Business magazines: Fortune, Business Week, Nation's Business, Forbes.
Major newspapers: New York Times, Wall Street Journal, Washington Post, Washington Star.
Daily newspapers (69) and weekly newspapers (192) in the service areas of American Electric Power's seven operating companies.
Daily newspapers (4) in Western coal-producing areas.
Technical publications: Science, Spectrum.

Results: Rarely, if ever, has an advertising campaign generated greater awareness of a public interest issue or earned more comments in the press.

While no formal measurement of audience reaction was undertaken, continuous surveys revealed extremely high readership ratings. The flood of mail received by the company, the number of extensive articles and editorials in magazines and newspapers, plus public comments by Washington officials indicated clearly that the advertising messages were hitting their mark.

Initially public reaction, expressed in direct mail to the company, was more negative than favorable, but this reversed at about midway in the campaign. Press coverage was largely negative or skeptical throughout. Support by the financial and business communities continued strong from the beginning.

Part of the campaign was devoted to a pre-existing controversy over the use of scrubbers -- strongly favored by the U.S. Environmental Protection Agency for the removal of SO_2 from power plant stack gases. The company took the position that scrubber technology was unproven and further that they were a potential source of land pollution. This company position provoked a counterattack by EPA.

Three advertisements published in 1975 invited reader response and comment. Replies totaled over 15,000. By a margin of nearly 15 to 1, they favored the company's viewpoint.

This astonishing margin provides one reliable norm for measuring the success of the campaign which, remember, initially elicited negative response. It is a clear indication that the audience had become better informed of the reasons for, and the potential consequences of, the energy crisis -- and had become more totally aware of the fundamental steps necessary to its solution.

A growing number of U.S. corporations have since begun speaking out on public interest issues through the use of paid space and air time. It could be concluded that the AEP advertising campaign gave encouragement to business to express its views on issues of public importance.

Advertisement reproduction Courtesy of American Electric Power Systems.

122

Are we blind to the real energy crisis?

The sad answer to that question could be yes. Unless we are aware of these facts:

By mid 1975 all industry in America, including electric utilities, must comply with the standards of the Clean Air Act. There is a possibility of a permissable extension to mid '76.

But whether it be '75 or '76, for many utilities there is no way on God's green earth that the present sulfur-dioxide emission standards can be met.

The "stack gas scrubber" that some say is the answer to removing sulfur-dioxide, doesn't exist in a practical working sense.

If such scrubbers did exist they couldn't be installed in time.

If they did exist and could be installed, the resulting ground pollution would be worse than any potential air pollution.

It is absolutely imperative that the Clean Air Act be amended. There is no other way.

The courts have already made it impossible for any government agency — including the Environmental Protection Agency — to grant a last minute reprieve.

Unless the Clean Air Act is amended we will have a *real* energy crisis.

And unless some responsible corporation brings these facts to light, this country of ours could be headed into chaos.

And shedding light is the sole purpose of this advertisement.

America has more coal than the Middle East has oil. Let's dig it!

American Electric Power System

Appalachian Power Co., Indiana & Michigan Electric Co., Kentucky Power Co., Kingsport Power Co., Michigan Power Co., Ohio Power Co., Wheeling Electric Co.

American Forest Institute

1974-1975

Objective: To convince a large segment of the American
public that America's forests can support present
and future wood and paper product needs as well
as provide benefits of their wooded state, if:

        a) Public and individually-owned woodlands
and forests are managed to the same
degree as industry-owned lands;

        b) Sufficient forest land is dedicated to
the growing of trees for harvest as
a primary objective;

        c) Wood fiber that is harvested is utilized
to the greatest degree through efficient
product specification and through
recycling.

Two other objectives of the campaign were to convince
priority audiences that the forest products industry
can meet reasonable air and water standards and
progress is being made to show that proper incen-
tives are needed for maximum recycling to utilize
fiber and solid waste more effectively.

Execution: Approach was thoroughly structured and divided into
carefully planned phases. The executive staff of
the American Forest Institute worked in close collaboration with their advertising agency, Cole & Weber,
and with research organizations. Liaison was maintained with key institute members as well.

Preparation for the campaign included a series of
in-depth attitudinal research studies, to determine
public knowledge and feeling about the forest products
industry, during a period when concern about the
environment was high.

A series of nine "green papers" (individual advertisements numbered in sequence) was prepared by the
agency and approved by the Institute executives and
directors. Key strategic elements included the use
of a second color ink (green) for the background of
each advertisement, numbering the advertisements,
and using the "Tree Farm -- Trees. The renewable
resource." signature to all advertisements. Identi-
fication of the American Forest Institute was limited
to the last sentence of the body copy.

Media: Initially _Time_ (weekly newsmagazine), in order to
obtain maximum frequency in terms of available
budget, and therefore present a greater number of
subjects.

Henry David Thoreau was wrong.

We can have wood. And the woods, too.

Back in the 1850's, naturalist Henry David Thoreau predicted that Maine would become a treeless wasteland.

But he underestimated the ability of man and nature working together to renew the forest.

Today, Maine has the greatest percentage of forestland of any state in the Union.

Which proves that, with man and nature working together, our forests can last forever—and can be logged forever.

One example:

The Robert H. Gardiner forestland in Maine. Owned by the same family since 1754, it has yielded four timber harvests for generations since then. Yet, it still provides the wildlife habitat, watershed protection, recreation and the scenic splendor Thoreau talked about. We call it sharing the land through multiple use.

Another example: Much of the Great Southern forest that some said was "gone forever" back in the 1920's has been harvested at least once since.

Today, the Southern forest supplies about 50% of the pulp, 40% of the plywood and 30% of the lumber made in the U.S.

That's what good forest management is all about. The forest industry has already shown that it can produce twice as much wood fiber per acre as public lands.

That means developing superior tree strains, thinning, fertilizing, and harvesting like any good farmer.

It also means the same forest is providing recreation, wildlife habitat, scenic beauty, watershed protection and timber harvest.

Industry forestlands are already working double time. All landowners must do the same if we're going to meet the next generation's voracious demand for wood. (The U.S. Forest Service has said we're going to need nearly twice as much wood in 25 years.)

We can do it. If federal and state forestry agencies adequately manage 136 million acres of publicly-owned commercial forest.*

And if the four million private individuals—farmers and others who own 59% of the nation's commercial woodlands—manage their lands for increased timber productivity as well as recreation and wildlife.

We can have our wood. And our woods, too. If we act now.

If you'd like to find out more about America's renewable resource, write: American Forest Institute, Dept. N-13, P.O. Box 873, Springfield, VA 22150.

*Commercial forest is described as that portion of the total forest which is capable and available for growing trees for harvest. Parks, Wilderness and Primitive Areas are not included.

Trees. The renewable resource.

"By concentrating in one magazine with a high
average frequency, we got the largest single
element of readership among our key publics that
we could get." In the first 12 months of the
campaign, the nine different subjects were run a
total of 27 times, or slightly more often than
every two weeks.

In fall 1975, the campaign was extended to Newsweek
(also a weekly newsmagazine). The advertisements
ran from September 8 to November 3 of that year,
alternating between Time and Newsweek. Four new
advertisements were prepared for this second wave
of advertising.

Results: Readership recognition studies indicate that the
AFI advertisements score high in both "noted" and
"read most" measurements. 12,000 letters were
generated by the closing sentence inviting readers
to contact the Institute for additional information.

The campaign also attracted strong support from the
firms in the forestry and forest products industry.

Because of its success, the campaign has been continued,
and the advertisement shown is the thirteenth in
the series.

Advertisement reproduction Courtesy of American Forest Institute.

Union Carbide Corporation

1974 to present, continuing

Objective: To provide a "platform of fact," establishing
              Union Carbide's technological relationship with many
              social and economic aspects of U.S. society, and
              hence its right to a voice in public affairs.

              Periodically, to extend from the "platform of fact"
              to express a company position concerning a question
              of controversy, in the context of other opinions.

Execution: Conventional relationship between Union Carbide
              and its agency, Young & Rubicam International, Inc.
              Subject areas are defined by Union Carbide (with
              involvement of top management) and prepared by
              Y&R as advertisements. Public opinion concerning
              product and economic sectors in which the company
              is involved is monitored through omnibus surveys
              conducted by the Opinion Research Corporation,
              custom-tailored research projects, and material
              from the "Public Demand" surveys of the Yankelovich,
              Skelly & White organization.

Media: News magazines (Time) and up-scale special-interest
              consumer magazines (New Yorker, Psychology Today,
              Smithsonian, Scientific American, etc.).
              Television: sponsorship (first Monday of each
              month) of CBS Evening News with Walter Cronkite.

              Periodic use of full-page advertisements to present
              a range of opinions concerning current social and
              economic issues: full-page advertisements (illus-
              trated) restricted to the New York Times and
              Washington Post and newspapers in key plant
              communities.

Results: Public response, as monitored by the research
              services used by Union Carbide, is strongly
              positive to both print and television advertisements.

              The magazine advertising was chosen as "the best
              campaign of 1975" by Advertising Age's columnist
              specializing in comment on print advertisements.
              He put particular emphasis on the effectiveness
              of the campaign theme, "Today, something we do
              will touch your life."

Advertisements reproduction Courtesy of Union Carbide.

CLIENT: UNION CARBIDE
PRODUCT: CORPORATE
TITLE: "PETRO CHEMICALS"

LENGTH: 60 SECONDS
COMM. NO.   UCCP5056
DATE: 7/9/75

1. (MUSIC THROUGH-OUT) ANNCR: (VO) Most of America's oil goes into gas tanks and

2. furnaces. But did you ever think what would happen

3. if someone carried off everything you own that's made

4. with the Petro Chemicals that come from oil.

5. (MUSIC)

6. (MUSIC)

7. (MUSIC)

8. (MUSIC)

9. (MUSIC)

10. (MUSIC)

11. (MUSIC)

12. (MUSIC)

13. (MUSIC)

14. At Union Carbide, one of our most important jobs is turning oil

15. into the Petro Chemicals that go into hundreds of little things

16. that make a big difference in your life.

17. So we have a serious stake in any decision that concerns oil.

18. And come to think of it, so do you.

19. Union Carbide.

20. Today, something we do will touch your life.

"Is it really true that there are fewer jobs for Americans as U.S. companies open plants overseas?"

William F. Gorog
Deputy Assistant to the President for Economic Affairs.

"Foreign investment results in a net creation of jobs for U.S. workers.

"The Federal Government has conducted studies regarding the effects of U.S. overseas plants on employment in this country. The preponderance of the evidence indicates convincingly that U.S. foreign direct investment in plants and equipment abroad provides jobs for workers here. For example, U.S. firms manufacture components for further processing or assembling in foreign plants and sale abroad. We produce capital equipment for use in foreign plants owned by U.S. parent companies. Additionally, jobs are provided for workers in U.S. home offices who provide support services for the foreign operations, for technical personnel providing engineering and similar services, and for research and development activities supported by foreign sales.

"Furthermore, because of trade barriers some foreign countries place on U.S. products, many markets are not open to us unless we invest directly in those countries.

"In summary, we believe there is strong evidence that more jobs are created than lost in the United States as a result of U.S. multinational companies investing overseas."

Rev. Howard Schomer
United Church Board for World Ministries.

"No one can be sure whether the opening of U.S. plants abroad, involving some closings at home, means less or more jobs for Americans than there otherwise would have been. Estimates range from a loss of 1.3 million jobs to a gain of half a million. The business of transnational corporations and their suppliers, both at home and abroad, has grown as they have responded to the requirement by many foreign countries that a larger portion of their production be done locally.

"But the effect of these plant shifts on jobs involves more than numbers. The U.S. Congress should act to protect workers at home and workers overseas from the harsher consequences of such transnational corporation moves. American workers, like those of West Germany and Japan, should be retrained or relocated when their jobs vanish because a certain production unit has been exported, and they should be assured an adequate income during the transition. Companies should be required to pay their overseas workers, especially in the Third World, in proportion to the value added by their labor rather than the miserable wages that mass unemployment and callous local governments often permit. Only then will American workers be reasonably safeguarded against the competition of cheap and exploited foreign labor."

Nat Goldfinger
Director Department of Research, AFL-CIO

"The unregulated export of American technology, capital and jobs has had a devastating impact on the American economy, workers and society. It has resulted in the shutdown of American production and its reestablishment abroad where foreign markets are served and exports to the U.S. are manufactured. Sales of foreign manufacturing subsidiaries of U.S. companies, in recent years, have been more than twice as great as the total volume of manufactured exports from the U.S. The shutdown of American manufacturing operations and the transfer of technology and capital erode America's industrial base; they depress the economy by the loss of jobs, payrolls, national tax revenues, local purchasing power, local taxes. The adverse impacts are tougher on workers than on capital or top management, who are much more mobile. Workers have great stakes in the American economy, their jobs and their communities."

***Global Reach*, by Richard J. Barnet & Ronald E. Muller, p. 301-2. Simon & Schuster, N.Y. 1974.**

"The dislocation global corporations cause by closing factories in the United States and opening them somewhere else is obvious. On computer tapes, jobs may be interchangeable. In the real world, they are not. A total of 250,000 new jobs gained in corporate headquarters does not, in any political or human sense, offset 250,000 old jobs lost on the production line. The changing composition of the work force and its changing geographical location brought about by the globalization of U.S. industry, are affecting the lives of millions of Americans in serious and largely unfortunate ways."

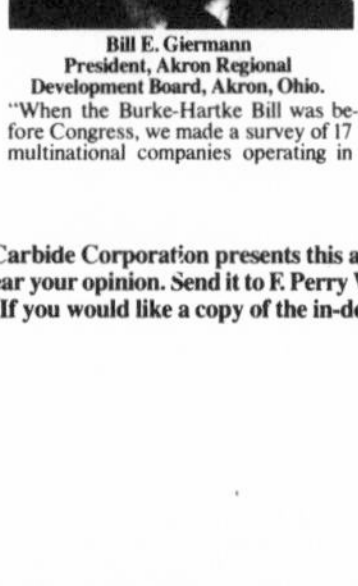

Bill E. Giermann
President, Akron Regional Development Board, Akron, Ohio.

"When the Burke-Hartke Bill was before Congress, we made a survey of 17 multinational companies operating in this area, and found that if the bill, which would have restricted the international business of American Companies, was passed it would eventually force these firms to eliminate 6,500 area jobs, or 10.6% of their combined workforce. The jobs lost would be those depending in some way on the overseas operations of locally-based multinational companies, supplying equipment, materials, research or administrative services for them. At that time it was estimated that such a job loss would, among other things, decrease yearly retail sales by over $32 million, and eventually force out of business an estimated 130 retail establishments in the Akron area."

I. W. Abel, President
United Steelworkers of America.

"When an American company opens a plant overseas it does not employ American workers. It employs people who live where the plant is located and often pays them substandard wages. Everytime an American company closes down its U.S. operation and relocates overseas, more American workers lose their jobs.

"In brief, we are exporting American jobs, American technology and American capital. We are also exporting our American standard of living. To protect and preserve our American standard of living, we must expand our economy, create jobs for more Americans and consume what Americans produce. The less American products we buy, the more American jobs are going to be eliminated. It's as simple as that. We depend upon each other for our jobs.

"Keep this in mind: 1. If American plants continue to locate overseas and flood our counters and showrooms with foreign made products, the American worker is going to continue to lose job opportunities to a foreign worker. 2. If no one buys what you produce or the service you sell, just how long do you think your job will last?"

Prof. Robert G. Hawkins
N.Y.U. Graduate School of Business Administration.

"Contrary to the more extreme allegations of organized labor, that multinational corporations have displaced or 'exported' many American jobs, industries with the highest investment abroad have had, on average, the fastest growth in American employment and production.

"It has been argued that production and employment in particular fields might have been still higher had there been less foreign investment. In a few isolated cases, perhaps they would. But the hard evidence...is that sectors with heavy foreign investment have significantly outperformed those with lower foreign investment—in growth rate of U.S. sales, in exports, and in employment. Whether this growth might have been still higher with less foreign investment can never be known with certainty. We can't run the world again to find out."

John H. Dent,
Representative, Pa.

"Yes. Not only are there fewer jobs in the United States as a consequence of U.S. companies moving overseas, but the job loss occurs in the production, or labor intensive, sector of the economy, which is by far the most important. Those who contend that there is no job loss, merely a 'transfer' of workers from production jobs to 'service' jobs, overlook a number of things, foremost of which is the large number of jobs presently being provided in labor intensive industries in the U.S., and second, the direct dependence of hundreds of American towns and cities on manufacturing plants engaged in labor-intensive production of goods.

"When multinationals make a corporate decision to transfer their labor intensive facilities abroad, usually to low wage areas, there is most assuredly job displacement. Some workers may be able to adjust by a painful process of reeducation and relocation, if such opportunities are available. More often than not, these workers come to depend on government payments like social security, trade adjustment assistance, and similar aid programs. The communities multinationals leave behind do not recover so easily either. The closing of plants and the loss of employment seriously undermines the economic base of these communities and diminishes the means which they have available for providing social and municipal services necessary for the well-being of their citizens."

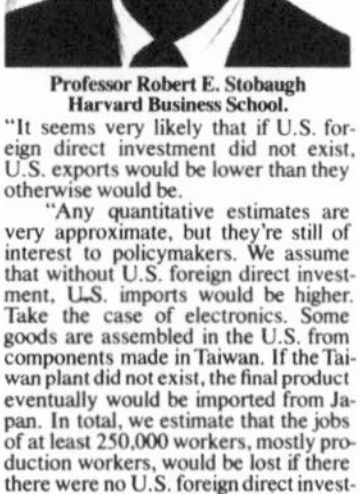

Professor Robert E. Stobaugh
Harvard Business School.

"It seems very likely that if U.S. foreign direct investment did not exist, U.S. exports would be lower than they otherwise would be.

"Any quantitative estimates are very approximate, but they're still of interest to policymakers. We assume that without U.S. foreign direct investment, U.S. imports would be higher. Take the case of electronics. Some goods are assembled in the U.S. from components made in Taiwan. If the Taiwan plant did not exist, the final product eventually would be imported from Japan. In total, we estimate that the jobs of at least 250,000 workers, mostly production workers, would be lost if there there were no U.S. foreign direct investment. Another 250,000 jobs exist in the main offices of U.S. multinationals because of direct foreign investment. This, plus an additional allowance for supporting workers, gives a total of perhaps 600,000 jobs."

Matthew J. Rinaldo
Representative, N.J.

"Not necessarily. Statistics rel
the Department of Commerce
dicated that, in the past, the c
employment rate among U.S.
tional companies increased fa
that for all U.S. companies.

"But no statistics tell th
truth. Any mass exportation
jobs represents a clear danger
ican labor and the U.S. econ
should avoid such a policy. T
gress should make it clear that
a plant abroad purely to cut lab
at home and increase profits
and unjustified.

"The United States has a
of living higher than most c
Naturally, foreign labor is chea
U.S. industry owes its succes
labor force, just as labor owe
ord high wages to U.S. indus
partnership between labor ar
try should be kept strong and ir

F. Perry Wilson, Chairman o
Board, Union Carbide Corpo

"No. Union Carbide's foreig
ments have resulted in a net
in U.S. jobs—2,500 of them o
last two decades. Furthermore
ous surveys have indicated thi
throughout most of American i

"Union Carbide manuf
abroad to serve markets abro
have only one exception inv
small investment in an assemb
tion which actually has saved
American jobs. Furthermore,
Carbide has never made a sig
manufacturing investment abro
it became unfeasible to supply c
markets through export from
In certain areas, with some p
we simply cannot compete c
from our U.S. plants.

"Union Carbide has cond
in-depth study of its internat
perience, covering a 24-year
1951-1974. The result: we fou
the foreign investments of
Carbide benefit U.S. employm
U.S. economy, and the U.S. ba
payments.

"Specifically, we found t
foreign investments have dire
ated 2,500 additional jobs in t
chiefly in the manufacturing a
bution areas. The truth is tha
Union Carbide installs a plant o
a decided "pull effect" develo
mand is stimulated for related p
—and exports increase. This pu
is tangible, measurable, and pre
As a result of our foreign inve
our export sales increased by a
one billion dollars during the pe
studied. Significant, too, was
Carbide's net positive contrib
the U.S. balance of payments
the last ten years which amou
1.6 billion dollars.

"No, foreign investments
destroy American jobs. They
them. At Union Carbide, we h
facts and the experience to pro

Union Carbide Corporation presents this advertisement in order to reflect a cross-section of opinion on a subject of general concern.
We would like to hear your opinion. Send it to F. Perry Wilson, Chairman of the Board, Union Carbide Corporation, 270 Park Avenue, New York, N.Y. 10017.
If you would like a copy of the in-depth study conducted by Union Carbide, Mr. Wilson will be glad to send it to you.

Hold your breath for 60 seconds.

Try this little experiment and chances are you'll find the last few seconds unbearable.

That desperate, terrifying sensation is caused by a lack of oxygen and an excess of carbon dioxide.

People with emphysema or other lung diseases know the feeling well. They live with it 24 hours a day.

Oxygen therapy can help many of them. But it can also sentence them to a bleak existence—living in fear, bound to heavy, bulky oxygen tanks.

Union Carbide has developed a portable oxygen system.

We call it the Oxygen Walker. It's small enough to be carried on a shoulder strap and weighs only 11 pounds full. Yet, incredibly, this handy pack can supply over 1000 liters of oxygen gas—enough for 8 hours or more, depending on individual flow rates.

Taking the Oxygen Walker with them, patients are free to leave their homes. Free to go walking, shopping, fishing... many have even returned to work.

The Oxygen Walker is only one of the things we're doing with oxygen. We supply more of it than anyone else in the country. For steelmaking, hospitals, wastewater treatment and the chemical industry.

But, in a way, the Walker is the most important use of our oxygen. Because to the people who use it, it is the breath of life.

UNION CARBIDE

Today, something we do will touch your life.

Atlantic Richfield Company (Arco)

1974 to present, continuing

Objective: To stimulate the public's interest in finding
              solutions for contemporary problems by inviting
              them to submit their own ideas. The campaign
              was originally tied to a long-term Atlantic
              Richfield interest, improvement of mass transit.
              By logical extension, the objective envolved to
              all kinds of societal improvements, for the long-
              term future. "America will change a great deal
              by the year 2076. Tell us what you think those
              changes should be."

Execution: The campaign was generated as one of a number of
              projects undertaken by Atlantic Richfield; the
              concept was submitted and executed by Arco's
              agency, Needham, Harper & Steers, Los Angeles.
              The campaign has been worked out via regular contact
              between departments within Arco and the agency,
              and top-level involvement at the approval stage.
              While now a part of long-term Arco advertising
              strategy, the "Tricentennial" concept was a happy
              discovered which emerged from the responses to the
              initial mass-transit "ideas" approach.

Media: Spot television, daily newspaper, national magazines,
              and Sunday newspaper magazine supplements (e.g.
              Parade, New York Times Sunday Magazine).in the
              Arco production, refining and retail marketing
              areas, plus major "influence" markets.

Results: In the first seven months of the mass-transit
              campaign, Arco received 35,000 ideas, generally
              accompanied by significant comment on the problems
              concerned. "Tricentennial" responses in four
              months exceeded 50,000.

              Research concerning effectiveness of the Public
              Transportation campaign in key markets showed a
              very high degree of awareness and approval. Strong
              public response to both campaigns proved that
              objectives had been met.

Advertisements reproduction Courtesy of Atlantic Richfield Company.

Public Transportation that runs more on ingenuity than gas.

Frederick L. Westover, Tuscaloosa, Alabama
The Flywheel Flash

Professor Westover suggests this idea to keep transportation rolling Equip buses with flywheels and electric motor-generators to start them spinning. The flywheel would store up enough energy to power the bus. One of man's oldest inventions could be the newest solution for our transportation problems.

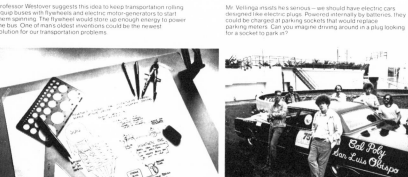

Ray Vellinga, San Diego, California
The Parkway Plug

Mr. Vellinga insists he's serious — we should have electric cars designed like electric plugs. Powered internally by batteries, they could be charged at parking sockets that would replace parking meters. Can you imagine driving around in a plug looking for a socket to park in?

D.E. Woodburn, Chula Vista, California
"The Solar Solution"

Mr. Woodburn thinks what we need to do is use solar energy to convert water, through electrolysis, into hydrogen fuel. Then we can run our cars on that instead of gas. Pollution free. He figures we could adapt our conventional cars for about $500 per car. That would involve a fuel supply tank filled with powdered and granular magnesium to hold the hydrogen. Plus, an adapter for the carburetor.

James M. Bready and Dr. William B. Stine, San Luis Obispo, California
The Sewer-Gas Special

Engineering students at California Polytechnic State University have been testing a 1966 Cadillac Fleetwood Brougham powered by sewer-gas. The idea is to develop a sewer-gas powered mini-bus system for small non-industrial cities. This way the city would be provided with a transportation system free from dependence on any petroleum-based product. And to use a source of fuel that is now totally wasted.

These are among the nearly 30,000 ideas on public transportation submitted to Atlantic Richfield Company. It's not our intention to endorse ideas. Our objective since the beginning has been simply this: To get you thinking about public transportation.

Please note that all ideas submitted become public property without compensation and any restriction on use or disclosure. IDEAS, P.O. Box 30169, Los Angeles, CA 90030.

Petroleum Products of
AtlanticRichfieldCompany

Atlantic Richfield invites you on a journey into the future.

The Tricentennial

America will change a great deal by the year 2076.

We have always been a nation more interested in the promise of the future than in the events of the past.

Somehow, the events of the past few years have made us doubt ourselves and our future.

Here at Atlantic Richfield, however, we see the future as an exciting time. The best of times. And we know that all of us can achieve a splendid future by planning for it now.

We'd like your help. We need your vision. We want you to tell us about the changes you

would like to see take place in America—and in our American way of life.

For example:

What ideas do you have for making life more fun than it is now?

What changes would you like to see in government? (City? State? Federal?)

What do you envision as the best way to solve our energy problems?

What about the future of business? (More regulation by government? Less?)

What measures would you take to protect the environment?

Or, if those topics don't appeal to you, pick one that does.

How should our physical world be altered? Do you recommend that we live underground? In plastic bubbles?

Will family life change? Will we choose a spouse by computer? Will divorce become illegal?

Tell us what you think those changes should be.

What should our schools be like? Should machines replace teachers?

What will make us laugh? What will be funny that isn't funny now?

What new major sports would you like to see? Three-dimensional chess? Electronic billiards?

Whatever your idea may be, we want to know about it. Write it. Draw it. Sing it. But send it.

In about six months we plan to gather your responses, analyze them, and make a full report

on what we've found out. We believe the report will provide a fascinating and valuable view of America's hopes, dreams, fears, and visions. We'll make sure it reaches the people who are in positions to consider and act on it.

Along the way we will make television commercials and newspaper and magazine ads out of many of the ideas so you can see what other people are thinking.

Please note that all ideas submitted shall become public property without compensation and free of any restriction on use and disclosure.

Send your idea to:
Tricentennial
Atlantic Richfield Company
P.O. Box 2076
Los Angeles, CA 90053

ARCO

AtlanticRichfieldCompany

Celebrate America's Tricentennial 100 years early.

Du Pont

(E. I. du Pont de Nemours & Company)

1975

Objective: Under conditions of serious public concern,
to take a public position concerning fluorocarbon
gases, of which Du Pont is a principal (and best-
known) producer. A scientific paper published
in 1974 had alleged that discharge of fluorocarbons
from refrigeration, aerosol propellants (spray can
products), and foam-blowing agents rose into the
upper atmosphere of the earth and depleted the
ozone layer, increasing exposure to ultra-violet
wavelengths of sunlight on the earth's surface.

Du Pont's objective was to state available information as objectively as possible and establish its
own position as a company handling this question
in a responsible manner.

Execution: While the fluorocarbon communications program was
perceived as of top management concern, management
of the effort was retained by the Freon Products
Division of the Organic Chemicals Department.
A steering committee headed by the division manager,
with representatives from marketing, research, legal,
advertising and public affairs departments, guided
the effort. Advertising was assigned to the agency
(N. W. Ayer) which regularly handles the division's
product advertising assignments, in the interest
of speed and technical background required.

High-level commitment to the position advanced in
the advertising was indicated by having the first
message signed by the Chairman of the Board, the
first time in Du Pont history. The first advertisement was produced and published within two weeks
time. A second advertisement, inviting comment
and information requests, was published three months
later.

The advertisements were part of a larger public
communications effort, coordinated by the Public
Affairs Department, with staff assistance and counsel
from Hill & Knowlton, Inc.

Because of the nature of the project, 21 different
departmental and management clearances were required
for the approval of each advertisement prior
to publication.

Media: First advertisement: key daily newspapers (Wall Street
Journal, New York Times, San Francisco Chronicle,
Los Angeles Times-Mirror, Chicago Tribune, Washington
Post, Wilmington News, Corpus Christi Caller-Times)
and two trade publications, Aerosol Age and
Editor & Publisher.

You want the ozone question answered one way or the other. So does Du Pont.

And most scientists agree there is time to find the answer.

Fluorocarbons are liquids and gases used in refrigeration, for air conditioning, and as propellants in about half the aerosol spray cans sold in this country. Some say that these useful, normally safe compounds will cause a health hazard by attacking the earth's ozone layer. We believe this is an oversimplification.

The point is, to date there is no conclusive evidence to prove this statement. To understand, then, why there is a controversy, it is necessary to unsimplify the issue. We must treat the real world on its own terms, and they are complex.

The model that raised the question.

Ozone is continually created and destroyed by natural forces scientists are seeking to understand. The ozone depletion theory, based on a computer model of the stratosphere, was reported in 1974 by two chemists at the University of California. This mathematical model calculates how fluorocarbons and the other fluorocarbon manufacturers are funding independent technological investigations in universities and research laboratories. Under the direction of acknowledged scientific experts, this research is designed to either prove or disprove the assumptions most important to the computer case against fluorocarbons.

Some research has been carried out since the model

in the stratosphere behave under the influence of a series of variables (such as tempera-

ture, altitude, sunlight, chemical concentration) to affect the ozone layer.

In order to estimate hypothetical reactions, and because little is actually known about the real ones, the modelers made a number of assumptions about the way the upper atmosphere behaves.

The unmeasured yardstick.

Before any judgments can be made using this model as a stratospheric yardstick, its accuracy must be determined.

Does it describe the real, three-dimensional world? To find this out, the validity of the modeler's basic assumptions must be determined.

Turning assumptions into facts.

Before a valuable industry is hypothesized out of existence, more facts are needed. To get these facts Du Pont and the other fluorocarbon manufacturers are funding independent technological investigations in universities and research laboratories. Under the direction of acknowledged scientific experts, this research is designed to either prove or disprove the assumptions most important to the computer case against fluorocarbons.

Some research has been carried out since the model was first presented. Scientists now have a better idea of the accuracy of the assumptions in the model.

ASSUMPTION: The ozone-depleting reaction with chlorine from fluorocarbons takes place at a rate that demands an immediate decision on fluorocarbon use.

FACT: Recent determinations of reaction rates disclose that the ozone/chlorine reaction actually takes place at a slower rate than that assumed by the model. In addition, the same research has shown that the reaction of chlorine with stratospheric methane proceeds at a faster rate. Since this reaction tends to remove chlorine from the ozone layer, the net effect of both reactions is to lessen the originally-calculated impact of fluorocarbons. In fact, the impact was overstated by 300%.

RESEARCH: To guide future measurements of stratospheric reactions, a laboratory program has been funded to measure the reactions of chlorine compounds and ozone under simulated stratospheric conditions.

Most scientists agree there is time to conduct the research needed to settle the controversy one way or the other... before a final decision is made on fluorocarbon production and use.

ASSUMPTION: There is no other way to get fluorocarbons out of the atmosphere except by the ozone-depleting reaction.

FACT: One well-known class of chemical reactions not considered in the model is that of chlorine compounds in the atmosphere in heterogeneous reactions.

In an article in SCIENCE (Feb. 14, 1975), Professors S. C. Wofsy, M. B. McElroy, and N. D. Sze of Harvard University caution that "If additional removal processes could be identified... or if additional sinks could be identified for stratospheric odd chlorine, the atmospheric and biological impacts of [fluorocarbons] would be reduced accordingly."

RESEARCH: Atmospheric chemistry involving ion molecule reactions has been described in recent months by several investigators. Reaction rates with ion molecules are known to be extremely fast and are believed to occur primarily in the lower atmosphere. Thus, ion molecules could react with fluorocarbons, allowing them to be removed from the atmosphere.

ASSUMPTION: Fluorocarbons are the only significant source of chlorine available for interaction with ozone in the stratosphere.

FACT: Many chlorine-containing materials are present in the atmosphere in varying concentrations. Of particular significance, large amounts of methyl chloride and carbon tetrachloride have been discovered in the troposphere and stratosphere.

In addition, new calculations on the injection of gaseous chlorine compounds into the stratosphere from volcanic eruptions have shown this as a significant contributor of chlorine not taken into account by the model.

RESEARCH: Scientists are completing an inventory of

chlorine-containing compounds in the atmosphere. It must be determined how nature deals with chlorine from these natural sources, before it can be shown that chlorine from fluorocarbons might pose a threat to the ozone layer.

Additional research.

A fluorocarbon industry research program is funding the development of a computer model that will better reflect the complex chemistry of the stratosphere.

In addition, other studies are under way to broaden our understanding of the total ozone production/destruction balance. These will concern themselves with other stratospheric reactions affecting ozone.

A panel of highly qualified academic scientists will advise on the technical programs covering various facets of the problem. This panel of independent experts will review the projects, providing a critical opinion on the pertinence of each, the probability of their success, and the completeness of the overall investigation.

Conclusion.

Much more experimental evidence is needed to evaluate the ozone depletion theory. Fortunately, as most scientists agree, there is time to gather this evidence. Du Pont has joined with other fluorocarbon manufacturers to provide funds for work by independent university scientists. Governmental agencies are also conducting research to help in the assessment of the theory.

Should the theory be proven correct after all the evidence is in, Du Pont, as we have stated, will stop the manufacture and sale of the offending compounds.

In the meantime, we believe that to act without the facts—whether it be to alarm consumers, or to enact restrictive legislation—is irresponsible. Final decisions cannot be made with only the information at hand.

The independent research described is presently being carried out by scientists at the following institutions:

Cambridge University—England
Environmental Research and Technology, Inc.
Massachusetts Institute of Technology
State University of New York
The Battelle Memorial Institute
The University of Reading—England
University of California
University of Denver
University of Illinois
University of Maryland
University of Michigan
Washington State University
York University—Canada
Xonics, Inc.

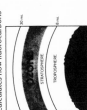

QUPONT

Second advertisement: a shortened list of
daily newspapers (<u>Wall Street Journal</u>, <u>New York
Times</u>, <u>Washington Post</u>) and <u>Editor & Publisher</u>,
plus a list of up-scale consumer magazines
reaching technically and intellectually oriented
readers: <u>Nature</u> (U.K. magazine in which the
initial scientific paper appeared), <u>Science</u>,
<u>Natural History</u>, <u>Scientific American</u>, <u>Washingtonian</u>,
<u>Atlantic Monthly</u>, <u>Harper's</u>, <u>New Leader</u>, <u>New Republic</u>,
<u>More</u>, <u>National Review</u>, <u>The Progressive</u>, and <u>New
York Review of Books</u>.

Results: Advertising readership, measured by the Starch
syndicated service, scored high. Information
offer in the second advertisement produced a
significant number of inquiries.

The controversy is yet to be resolved. It will
continue to ebb and flow with the tides of scientific
research into the fluorocarbon/ozone theory.
Du Pont believes, however, the advertisements
have helped communicate its position on the issue
to the public.

<u>Advertisement reproduction Courtesy of E. I. du Pont de Nemours
& Company</u>.

The ozone layer vs. the aerosol industry. Du Pont wants to see them both survive.

Fact.

At heights from eight to thirty miles above the earth are concentrations of ozone which block out some ultraviolet wavelengths of sunlight. The ozone is continually destroyed and formed by processes and reactions that scientists are seeking to understand and explain.

Theory.

Some fluorocarbon gases used in about half the aerosol spray products and in most refrigeration and air-conditioning systems may be the cause of some ozone depletion.

Controversy.

The current controversy centers around the theory. On one side are scientists, theorists, and some legislators who contend that these useful, inert gases, breaking down into chlorine, will lead eventually to an unnatural amount of ozone depletion.

On the other side are scientists, researchers, and the aerosol industry who maintain there is no persuasive evidence to support this recently-proposed theory of ozone depletion. And, they say, even if the theory has elements of correctness, other chemicals, reactions, and processes might be primarily responsible.

Why, they ask, should an industry be prejudged and useful fluorocarbon products be destroyed before any answers are found?

Du Pont's Position.

As the world's leading supplier of fluorocarbon propellants, Du Pont has an obvious stake in the outcome of the controversy. As a corporation, we are committed to making products safely, and to supplying safe products to our customers.

We have publicly announced that, should reputable evidence show that some fluorocarbons cause a health hazard through depletion of the ozone layer, we are prepared to stop production of the offending compounds.

To date there is no experimental evidence to support the contention that FREON and other similar compounds have caused a depletion of the ozone layer. In the 45 years since introducing our brand of fluorocarbons, FREON, we have spent hundreds of man years and many millions of dollars on research to study other toxicological and environmental safety aspects of these compounds.

Many scientists who have studied the ozone depletion theory agree that, even if the hypothesis is valid, no significant effect will occur during the three years needed to develop definitive information. A report by one of the early proponents says that recent laboratory studies indicate that the original ozone loss projections of the computer-derived hypothesis are at least three times too high. So it would appear that there is time to study.

The Evidence.

Perhaps we should say "the lack of evidence"—for that is what exists—on both sides of the controversy. Hypothesis lacks support. Claim meets counterclaim. Assumptions are challenged on both sides. And nothing is settled.

Nor will there be any hard answers until some hard facts are produced.

In the meantime, aerosol products suffer under a cloud of presumed guilt, and other fluorocarbon-dependent industries are seriously threatened. We believe this is unfair. The "ban now—find out later" approach thrust upon an $8 billion segment of industry in this issue, both in the headlines and in many legislative proposals, is a disturbing trend. Businesses can be destroyed before scientific facts are assembled and evaluated; and many might never recover. Even though these facts may vindicate them. Except where available evidence indicates that there may be immediate and substantial danger to health or environment, the Nation cannot afford to act on this and other issues before the full facts are known.

What Du Pont is Doing About It.

We are trying to find the truth. Du Pont and other fluorocarbon manufacturers are funding a $3 million to $5 million program coordinated by the Manufacturing Chemists Association to analyze whether or not fluorocarbons are affecting the ozone layer. This comprehensive study, by acknowledged scientific experts here and abroad, and concurrent Federal studies will include actual stratospheric research and experimentation. These studies should be concluded in about three years, and much useful information will be available in the interim.

In addition to helping study any effect of fluorocarbons on the ozone layer, Du Pont chemists and researchers are searching for new fluorocarbons in case of restrictive regulation on those under attack. We are preparing to discuss the progress of the research with our customers.

There are some who say that aerosols should be banned now even before the facts of the studies are known. Du Pont wants to do what is right—for people, for the aerosol industry, and for ourselves—but we believe sincerely there is time to gather information and make a reasoned decision.

Our Customers' Businesses.

Whatever the obstacles, we pledge our best efforts to develop and manufacture products that will meet the needs of those industries that depend on us today: for FREON. Aerosol packaging. Refrigeration. Air-conditioning. Fire-fighting. Etc.

We feel responsible to an industry we helped develop…to those marketers and contract fillers who have grown in the aerosol industry with Du Pont. We do not want to see their businesses destroyed by premature legislative action, regulations, or even managerial decisions, that are not based on fact.

Irving S. Shapiro

Chairman of the Board

There's a world of things we're doing something about.

Chase Manhattan Bank

1975 - 1976 and continuing

Objective: To speak out on a key issue affecting the
              U.S. economy and nation, and generate awareness
              and concern for what might happen if action is
              not taken.

              Specifically, Chase feels that "capital shortfall"
              (lack of capital at times needed for economic
              growth) is the single, most perilous problem which
              the U.S. faces. The advertisements proposed a six-
              point plan for the stimulation of capital formation.

Execution: Advertising was prepared by Doremus & Company, a
              Chase advertising agency, in close liaison with the
              bank's top management. A written strategy plan was
              developed, defining audience targets and campaign
              objectives. The initial pulse of the campaign was
              limited to three weeks, and to three different
              executions of the same theme.

Media: Three newspapers -- The Wall Street Journal, The New
              York Times, and The Washington Post -- together with
              three weekly newsmagazines, Time, Newsweek, and
              U.S. News & World Report, and two business magazines,
              Business Week (weekly) and Forbes (bi-weekly).

              A portfolio of advertisements was mailed to key
              business executives throughout the U.S., inviting
              their comments.

Results: Readership studies showed that the ads were seen and
              read by the target audience, and that the message
              was well received. Results were also measured in
              terms of the strong reaction to the advertisements:
              hundreds of letters, articles in newspapers discussing
              the campaign and the capital shortfall concept, re-
              prints of the campaign in company house organs, and
              similar kinds of implicit praise. The texts of the
              advertisements were reprinted by other companies in
              paid media, and were read into the Congressional Record
              of the U.S. Congress several times.

              The response to the initial campaign caused Chase to
              continue speaking out on the issue as part of their on-
              going bank advertising effort.

Advertisement reproduction Courtesy of Chase Manhattan Bank.

"Wolf!"

The Chase is crying "Wolf!" Again. And we mean it. Again.

America is faced with a shortage of capital. Capital vital to the healthy growth this nation must have if it is to maintain and improve the living standards of all Americans.

In 1952, we published a study warning against government disincentives to the continuing search for natural gas. We raised more caution flags in 1956, 1957, and 1961 about industry's ability to continue "to deliver low-cost petroleum energy."

We were accused of crying "Wolf!" at that time. And indeed we were. But it was no pretense.

Our warnings were based on hard facts which became even harder with every disappearing drop of cheap imported oil.

Today we face an equally hard set of facts regarding the level of capital formation and mounting capital needs:

Fact 1: The next ten years will require twice as much capital as the past ten.

Fact 2: It will take a tremendous effort of husbanding sources and resources — far more than it took to win World War II or to put a man on the moon.

Fact 3: We will be lucky if there is as much as $2.6 trillion for building and rebuilding our industrial capacity.

Fact 4: Set against the needs of $4.1 trillion, there'll be a shortfall of $1.5 trillion.

Which means we will be under-investing $400 million a day every day for the next ten years.

The highest priority of our economy right now should lie in the nurture and stimulation of capital formation. Because everything the American people need and want grows out of that.

How do we deal with the problem? Chase proposes a six-part action program:

• Provide sufficient inducements for an ever-growing base of personal savings.

• Establish more realistic guidelines for depreciation allowances.

• Give preferential tax treatment for retained corporate earnings used for investment purposes.

• Ameliorate our relatively harsh treatment of capital gains compared with that of most other countries.

• Stabilize our monetary and fiscal policies to prevent violent swings in the economy.

• Eliminate unnecessary controls. And do away with outmoded government regulations and agencies that restrict our free market economy.

Capital formation must be government's business, businesses' business, labor's business, banking's business — everybody's business.

Your business.

CHASE

Exxon Corporation

1975

Objective: To discuss, through separate advertisements, matters of national concern, such as Alaskan oil, coal, energy conservation, and corporate social responsibility.

    To communicate Exxon's commitment to be responsive to the social and environmental impact of its activities.

Execution: Exxon corporate advertisements are prepared by the McCaffrey & McCall advertising agency, working in close relationship with Exxon top management. "Tracking studies" are used to trace public opinion concerning the issues of petroleum and energy, and to study how the public perceives advertising messages on these subjects. (Studies are conducted four times a year, by Roger Seasonwein & Associates.)

Media: Television (65%) and magazines (35%), with a small amount of radio.

    Television has included sponsorship of NBC Saturday Night News, a single program of NBC Evening News once every other week, NBC Sunday Evening News, and the every-Sunday program, Meet The Press.

    Magazines used include Time, Newsweek, Reader's Digest, Atlantic Monthly, Harper's, and National Geographic.

Results: "Tracking studies" indicate high recall of advertisements, and high awareness of Exxon.

    The campaign was named "best corporate advertising campaign in the U.S." by the Saturday Review for 1975.

Advertisement reproduction Courtesy of Exxon Corporation.

McCAFFREY & McCALL INC.

CLIENT: EXXON CORP.

PRODUCT: EXXON

TITLE: "U.S. COAL RESERVES REV."

LENGTH: 60 SECONDS

COMMERCIAL NO: XONC6560

1. (MUSIC THROUGHOUT)
KILEY:(VO) Exxon has shown
you this map before

2. so you could see where the
world's oil is located.

3. Most of it is here in the
Middle East.

4. But now we'd like to change
the picture to show you what the
world looks like

5. if the size of each country
were in proportion to the coal
reserves under its land.

6. The United States would
become this big.

7. Because our country has almost one-third of the world's
coal reserves.

8. Europe and the Middle East
are small by comparison.

9. And if you look closer, you'll
also see that much of this coal
is in the West

10. where states like Montana,
Wyoming, and New Mexico
account for about 40 percent
of America's coal reserves.

11. If you add these deposits
to the coal in the rest of
the U.S.,

12. America comes out with
total coal reserves equal in
energy to twice the
Mid-East oil reserves.

13. And this is why Exxon is
hard at work to find better
ways to mine coal.

14. Cleaner ways to burn it.
And new ways to put it to
work.

15. (MUSIC OUT)

American Gas Association

1976 and continuing

Objective: To state the case for giving national
               priority to developing the resources of
               natural gas available to the U.S.
               To encourage consumers to conserve gas.

Execution: The advertisements are prepared by the
               account team of the J. Walter Thompson
               Company, working in close collaboration
               with the staff and committees of the
               American Gas Association. Decisions
               concerning approach, target audience, and
               subject matter are taken in terms of
               continuing studies of consumer attitudes.

Media: Wall Street Journal, newsmagazines,
               business magazines, network television.

Results: Not available.

Advertisement reproduction Courtesy of American Gas
Association.

JWT

420 LEXINGTON AVENUE
NEW YORK 17

CLIENT: AMERICAN GAS ASSN.
PRODUCT: NATURAL GAS
TITLE: "PIPELINE"
CODE NO.: AGAS 5256
JO#: 459607

DATE: 12/16/75
LENGTH: 60 SECONDS

 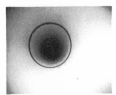 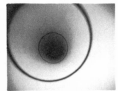 

1. (MUSIC AND EFFECTS) PRESENTER: This is Jim Fagan,

2. here to take you on an incredible journey

3. through the million-mile

4. network of underground pipes

 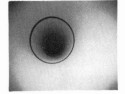  

5. that carry natural gas quickly

6. and quietly all over the country.

7. To this steel mill, for instance...

8. ...where gas is vital to making steel.

  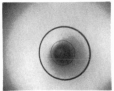 

9. America's industry depends on natural gas for half its energy.

10. Millions of jobs depend on gas. Maybe yours.

11. Natural gas also travels to forty million homes...

12. ...where families like this depend on gas heat to keep warm.

13. You know, gas is the most efficient of all the major energies.

14. Right now, there's a critical shortage of clean efficient gas energy,

15. and the gas industry's doing all it can to develop new supplies.

16. But much of this work waits on

 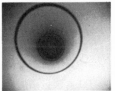  

17. the tough energy decisions America must make. And soon.

18. America's gas lines are her life lines.

19. That's why this country must get more gas.

20. (MUSIC)

145

The gas you save could save your job.

Right now our country's natural gas shortage is critical. The gas you save at home can help keep factories running, and help keep people working. Your own job might even depend on America's natural gas supply.

Natural gas provides half the energy for industry.

There'll be more gas energy to run America's factories if each and every one of us tries to save all the natural gas he can.

Turn your thermostat down. It makes a big difference.

If every family that has gas heat turned the thermostat down just four degrees, it would save enough gas to supply the entire United States food and lumber industries for a year. Use storm doors and windows, too, and use weather stripping where it's needed. Insulate your attic adequately to keep heat from escaping through the roof. Check your home for ways to save on natural gas. Remember, if we all save a little, America saves a lot.

Use gas wisely. It's clean energy for today and tomorrow. A⚡A American Gas Association

Tate & Lyle, Ltd. (I)

1949 - 1951

Objective: To fight the Labor Government's declared
               intention to nationalize industries where
               the market was controlled by only two or
               three companies. The list of commodity
               producers to be nationalized included the
               sugar industry. Tate & Lyle, Ltd., was
               by far the largest sugar company in the U.K.

Execution: Tate & Lyle chose to fight the government
               proposals on its own, while welcoming the support
               of other sugar companies. All decisions were
               taken at Board level. A cartoon character,
               "Mr. Cube," was conceived as as a non-human
               spokesman -- modeled on a pre-war symbol
               ("Mr. Therm") which had been used in gas company
               advertising. ("Mr. Cube" was created during a
               a meeting with an employers' association,
               Aims of Industry, and drawn in final form by
               a well-known artist, Bobby St. John Cooper.)
               Support was enlisted among the refinery and
               distribution workforce (7,500 workers), and
               competitions were run for slogan suggestions.
               All slogans used in the campaign were devised
               by employees.

Media: To avoid direct confrontation with the government,
               the campaign did not use direct space advertising.
               (Commercial radio and television were not
               available, and did not have to be considered.)

               The campaign was carried on Tate & Lyle sugar
               packages, presented on point-of-sale displays
               in retail shops, and communicated through a
               variety of promotional schemes. These included
               gadgets, such as an anti-nationalization dice game,
               and a set of 5 magnetic alphabet blocks which
               spelled TATES but could not be arranged to spell
               STATE. (This promotion was a favorite of Sir
               Winston Churchill.)

Results: Impact of the campaign built up slowly but
               cumulatively until the General Election of 1950,
               during which campaign the company was savagely
               attacked by two Labor Ministers. Abruptly, the
               Tate & Lyle campaign hit the front pages of the
               national press and became the subject of editorial
               opinions and cartoons. Identification of "Mr. Cube"

Sugar Package Advertising for Tate & Lyle, ca. 1949

reached so high a level, the <u>Evening Standard</u>
used a picture of "Mr. Cube" as the only
heading for their leading article on the campaign.
The attack was on the basis that "big business"
was engaging in politics and interfering with the
outcome of the election. Ironically, it was the
attack that put the campaign on the map and
dramatized the issue of whether or not nationalizat
is an efficient way of operating an industry.

The 1950 General Election reduced the Labor
majority sharply, and no major nationalization
was undertaken. The 1951 Election returned the
Conservatives to power. The considered opinion
of historians is that, by making the general
British public aware of nationalization's
shortcomings, the first Tate & Lyle "Mr. Cube"
campaign had an influence on this political
evolution.

<u>Advertisement reproduction Courtesy of Tate & Lyle, Ltd.</u>

" Well, wot is it *this* time—speeding, obstruction, illegal propaganda? "

Cartoon reactions to Tate & Lyle Campaign, ca. 1949–1951

Tate & Lyle, Ltd. (II)

1973 to present, and continuing

Objective: To present a position in the national interest
concerning sugar production, prices, and
supply, during a period when international
events put the company in an extremely difficult
position.

Initially (October, 1973), to state the case
against a movement to cut back cane sugar supplies
in favor of EEC sugar beetroot supplies, in
connection with the U.K. entry into the European
Common Market.

Thereafter, to explain an abrupt shortage in
sugar supplies, together with a rapid rise in
sugar prices, in the aftermath of the U.K.'s
entry into the EC, a worldwide failure of sugar
beet crops, and a rise in oil prices which
affected the price of production.

To contend with the problems of continuing to
employ the Tate & Lyle workforce during a period
of complicated supply and interrupted production.

To encourage public support of the British Government in its negotiations with the EC concerning
cane and beet sugar resources (importation vs.
production within the Community).

On a continuing basis, to maintain the company's
presence and right to a voice in the complex issues
of national and international management of
sugar supplies.

Execution: "Mr. Cube" (See Case Example, Tate & Lyle I) had
served as company corporate symbol from 1951, when
the nationalization issue was settled, to the time
when the cane/beet sugar issue arose. There was
initial skepticism about his relevance to the
new controversy, particularly since the company
had become widely diversified. He was elected
after close consultation between the company's
Board of Directors and the agency, KH Communications
Group, to lead the company attack during the
complex situation involving the EC and basic
sugar resources.

Basic identity was maintained throughout by
use of the artist who originated the "Mr. Cube"
visual concept in 1950, Bobby St. John Cooper.
While conventional relationships between
agency and client were maintained, the agency
account group dealt directly with the management
level of the company. A first campaign (tied
into the debate in the British Parliament)
concerning a motion in favor of cane supplies
was aborted when the Government withdrew its
resistance. Thereafter, in a volatile situation,
the "Mr. Cube" campaign was used to react on a
short-term basis to developments in sugar prices
and supply, and the employment implications for
Tate & Lyle's work force. A campaign ran through
the period explaining the company's diversifications.

Unless Britain acts now, soon all the sugar we eat could come from sugar-beet alone.

No more would be made from the sugar cane we've always enjoyed.

Which could mean closing down the Tate & Lyle refineries in London, Liverpool, and Greenock.

And losing *six thousand* people their jobs.

Not to mention the sugar workers in the developing Commonwealth countries which grow the cane, whose position could be perilous.

It could also mean a situation where there would be no competition and little choice.

Where the range of special sugar products like Caster Sugar, Golden Syrup, Icing Sugar, Black Treacle, and the Brown Sugars could be drastically reduced.

Where there would be no place for Mr Cube.

But it *would* mean prosperity all round for the Continental sugar-beet farmers. Paid for by the British housewife and tax-payer.

Issued by the Board of Tate & Lyle Limited on behalf of their customers, their suppliers, their employees and their shareholders.

153

In 1976 KH Communication Group, the agency throughout, placed Corporate color advertisements in the national press emphasizing the company diversification around the world and using quotes and pictures of foreign Government Ministers and public figures, as well as Mr. Cube. In addition to the ongoing corporate and financial advertising a new theme using color pages in the women's magazines and black and white large advertisements in the national press appeared, featuring Mr. Cube and Sheer Energy -- tying in with the Olympic Games.

Media:
National newspaper, to explain issues that are more complicated than can be communicated through other media.

The campaign has also appeared in other national press media (e.g. The Economist) in connection with an overall corporate campaign to explain company diversification and performance.

In 1976, women's magazines were added to the schedule, using color pages to present a new theme.

Results:
The "Mr. Cube" campaign, continuing since 1951 and readied to deal with the Parliament motion in favor of cane sugar supply, is considered to have had some influence on the Government's withdrawal of its objections. (Despite the fact that the campaign did not appear, and that the press space booked for it was used for general corporate advertising.)

Desite the serious condition of sugar supplies in mid-1974, the effectiveness of Tate & Lyle's advertising in explaining the situation and in establishing the company's diversification was demonstrated by the company's stock share performance. (V. Financial Times share price index, 1974.)

By late 1974, when the British Minister, Mr. Fred Peart, went to negotiate the sugar situation, the "Mr. Cube" advertisements supporting his efforts had such widespread recognition, they did not require a company signature. Peart's mission was successful. The "Mr. Cube" company symbol has been so well established that it is used in all Tate & Lyle advertising, not only corporate financial announcements, but also advertising to the British workforce through mass circulation newspapers (such as the Daily Mirror).

The "Mr. Cube" character, and the reputation of Tate & Lyle advertising for communicating complicated financial information, is now well-established. The company's advertisements command attention not only in the City but also on the shop-floor.

In 1975, a Tate & Lyle advertisement was given a Special Award in the London Times Corporate Advertising competition, as "the most novel, inventive, and original entry."

Advertisement reproduction Courtesy of Tate & Lyle, Ltd.

United Kingdom

Bristol Channel Ship Repairers, Ltd.

1975

Objective: To resist nationalization of this company, a
                small Welsh ship repairing company, in the
                interest not only of its stockholders, but also
                of the management and workers actively involved
                in maintaining its independence. B.C.S.R. was
                the smallest firm on the Government's list to
                be nationalized; it was also the only completely
                independent company on the list.

Execution: A campaign to resist nationalization was conceived
                and produced by Tim Miller and KH Advertising,
                working directly with client management at the
                Board Room level. The advertisements achieved a
                note of personal communication by addressing
                themselves directly to a Cabinet Minister, Mr.
                Anthony Wedgwood Benn.

Media: National newspapers, including daily newspapers
                generally regarded as the "popular press."

Results: Over 10,000 people wrote to the company; an
                unknown number sent coupons directly to the Prime
                Minister or to Mr. Benn. Shipowners all over
                the world expressed their support. In June,
                1975, Mr. Benn was moved to another ministry.
                Shortly afterwards the Bill was dropped.

                It was re-introduced in the 1975-1976 session,
                still including B.C.S.R. Whether B.C.S.R.
                will finally escape nationalization is still
                (as of July, 1976) not clear.

Advertisement reproduction Courtesy of Bristol Channel Ship
Repairers, Ltd.

Please, Tony, think again.

Don't nationalise us.

There are very good reasons why you should take us off your list of ship repairers. Here are some of them.

1. We're small. We're the smallest on your list. We represent some 2% of the people working in the industry, divided between six separate repair yards along 70 miles of coast.

2. We're efficient. We have nothing to do with ship **building**. We're specialists in ship **repairing**; and as you know, the best in Northern Europe. We're an independent company, the only one on your list. We've never needed Government money. Our productivity is nearly double the industry average. We've not lost an hour from labour troubles in seven years so we're trusted to do the job on time. Over 80% of our customers' business specially diverts to our docks and last year 62% of our total sales were in foreign earnings.

3. We're well on the way towards Workers Control. Already we have many employee directors. Already 20% of the company belongs to the employees. Already every worker – shop-floor, apprentices, employee directors, staff, shop stewards – receives regular up-to-date profit and loss figures and nearly all are shareholders. In time over half the shares will belong to the workers, the people who invest their labour in the company.

We've made a good start, but if you nationalise us this co-partnership will stop. The State will own the company, not our workers.

Some of us would see that as a move to the right, not to the left.

 # Bristol Channel Ship Repairers Ltd.

Fighting for co-partnership.

United Kingdom

British Government
Counter-Inflation Publicity Unit

1975-1976

Objective: To assist the Government as a whole in the presentation of its counter-inflation policies as approved by Parliament.

Execution: A special unit, the Counter-Inflation Publicity Unit, was organised and staffed to deal with the task. The Industrial Editor of the Daily Mirror was seconded as head of the Unit. Initial plan proposed in mid-summer 1975 was approved at Ministerial level. The advertising agency, Boase Massimi Pollitt, undertook a three-phase campaign based on research including focus-group interviews. First phase of the policy was announced by the Prime Minister, supported by an explanatory advertisement and a pamphlet distributed to every household presenting details Second phase was a series of advertisements, late 1975, consisting of leading industrialists and trade union leaders giving their reasons for supporting the fight against inflation. The third phase was to publicise a selective price restraint scheme addressed to shoppers.

Media: National and regional daily and Sunday newspapers. Television advertising and national press were in February/March, 1976, used for the third phase.

Results: Qualitative research indicated high attention to the advertisements in each of the three phases.

Advertisement reproduction Courtesy of the Central Office of Information.

It's catching on.

The red Price Check triangle is now on display in all sorts of shops up and down the country.

The red triangle means that certain products and services in those shops will not rise in price by more than 5p in the pound between now and the middle of August.

If you are not sure which products or services are included, please ask at the shops displaying the triangle.

It is because pay restraint is slowing down cost rises that so many shopkeepers and manufacturers have felt able to join with the Government in the Price Check scheme, even though many of them have seen their businesses and profits badly hit by inflation.

Inflation hurts us all. Price Check is one of the ways we are getting to grips with it, and a sign that we are making progress.

Inflation. We can beat it together.

ISSUED BY HER MAJESTY'S GOVERNMENT

159

France

Banque Nationale de Paris (BNP)

1975

Objective: To distinguish BNP from other banks. Since it is
             virtually impossible to distinguish one bank from
             another by selling its products or services, the
             copy line was taken which concentrated on the
             banking establishment itself. This led to a campaign
             stressing the role of leadership which the BNP plays
             in the French national economy, in the context of
             current trends.

Execution: Campaign was planned and executed by BNP's advertising
             agency, Publicis, together with the bank's marketing
             team. All advertisement subjects and plans were
             approved at top management level.

Media: National magazine (four-color), national newspaper. -

Results: Not available.

Advertisement reproduction 6ourtesy of Banque Nationale de Paris.

Les petites entreprises se transforment.

Mais elles n'ont pas encore résolu tous leurs problèmes d'équipement.

La France est ce qu'elle est. Ses entreprises sont à son image : diverses, équilibrées, humaines. Petites ou moyennes, 1.600.000 entreprises assurent ainsi une grande partie de la production industrielle, l'essentiel des activités commerciales, la totalité de l'artisanat.

La PME serait-elle pour autant une entreprise désuète, dont notre pays aurait le secret ? Au contraire. Aux Etats-Unis, pays des "géants" industriels, le nombre des petites entreprises va croissant. Partout, on redécouvre ses vertus : échelle humaine, dynamisme, esprit d'innovation et d'invention.

Innover, inventer, c'est-à-dire se développer, s'équiper. Pour cela, la petite ou moyenne entreprise a un partenaire, qui imagine des solutions adaptées à chaque problème, à chaque entreprise : la BNP. Elle y apporte son expérience de première

banque française.

La BNP fait plus encore, 4ème banque mondiale, elle fait bénéficier l'entreprise de son implantation et de ses contacts dans tous les pays. Avec la BNP, les petites entreprises peuvent, elles aussi conquérir de nouveaux marchés. La BNP financera leurs exportations.

Le monde redécouvre les PME. Aux PME de découvrir le monde.

Aider les PME à investir, c'est aussi le rôle de la BNP.

BNP

Quand la 4ème banque mondiale est française, chaque Français y trouve son compte.

France

IREB
(Institut de Recherches Scientifiques,
Economiques, et Sociales sur les Boissons)
1974 - 1975

Objective: In the effort to combat alcoholism, to
             offer an alternative to total abstinence
             through a concept of daily alcohol intake
             related to weight.

Execution: The IREB is sponsored by the major producers
             of aperitifs and liqueurs in France:
             Noilly Prat, Cointreau, Picon, Pernod,
             Remy-Martin, Dubbonet-Cinzano-Byrrh,
             Cusenier, Benedictine, Saint-Raphael,
             Ricard, and Martini & Rossi, and by the
             Chambre Syndicale des Importateurs de
             Gin & Whisky. The basic concept of the
             "information campaign" -- "Count your drinks.
             Seven drinks a day -- never more." -- was
             submitted to a council of management representatives
             of the participating firms. On the basis of
             their authorization, the series of cinema commercials
             and promotional devices were produced.

Media: Cinema: key cinemas in large and medium-sized
             cities.

             Informational material, including "Normalcool,"
             a cardboard calculator enabling automobile
             drivers to estimate their alcohol blood level
             as a function of sex, weight, and number of
             glasses consumed.

Results: Strong public response, basically affirmative.
             Strong resistance to the "seven glasses a day"
             concept on the part of the CNDCA (Comite National
             de Defense Contre l'Alcoolisme). High level
             of controversy has effectively dramatized the
             problem of alcoholism to the French public.

Case history based on an article in the International Herald
Tribune, October 17, 1975. (Illustrative material
not available.)

163

Germany

Gruner + Jahr AG & Co., Publishing House

1975

Objective: To explain, " in an amusing, factual, and
               therefore believable way, "the contribution
               of advertising and product development to
               the richness of contemporary German life.

Execution: Campaign was conceived by the advertising
               agency, Hildmann, Simon, Rempen & Schmitz
               (Düsseldorf), working with the Marketing
               Manager of Gruner & Jahr. Entire campaign
               (six advertisement subjects) was submitted to
               top Gruner & Jahr management approval.

Media: National consumer magazines: Brigitte, Capital,
               Eltern, Essen & Trinken, Gong, Schöner Wohnen,
               Stern.

               The campaign ran during September 1975. A
               brochure is available including the six
               double-page advertisements. One motif (see
               illustration) is available as a poster.

               Activity is part of on-going G & J programs,
               including exhibitions on social advertising,
               government advertising, etc.

Results: The advertisements were extremely well-
               received by the public. Advertisers and
               agencies praised the campaign highly.

Advertisement reproduction by courtesy of Gruner + Jahr AG & Co.

Schon vor 50 Jahren hat man über Konsumterror gestöhnt.

Genau wie heute gewisse Leute. Nicht mehr und nicht weniger.

Denn auch damals gab es schon welche, die nicht verstehen wollten, daß Menschen ein ganz natürliches Besitzstreben haben.

Das Bestreben, ein schöneres, bequemeres und angenehmeres Leben zu führen als ihre Vorfahren.

Damals wie heute brauchte man Werbung nicht, um zu verführen. Begehrens-

werte Sachen machen von selbst begehrlich.

Aber man brauchte Werbung, um zu zeigen, was es alles gibt. In welcher Vielfalt. In welcher Qualität. Zu welchen Preisen. Mit welchen Vorzügen.

Denn die wichtigste Aufgabe der Werbung in einer Wettbewerbsgesellschaft ist nicht, zu erreichen, daß man etwas kaufen sollte, sondern zu zeigen, was man alles kaufen kann.

Man nennt die Zwanziger Jahre auch die Goldenen Zwanziger. Zu Recht.

Denn bis dahin war es den Deutschen noch nie so gut gegangen.

Bis heute ist es den Deutschen noch nie so gut gegangen. Auch denen nicht, die heute stöhnen.

An welche Zeiten wollen die uns denn gewöhnen?

Und wie ist es heute?

Germany

Informationszentrale der Elektrizitaetswirtschaft
(Central Information Office for the Electricity Industry)

March-June, 1975 and Sptember-December, 1975

Objective: To explain the contribution of nuclear power
               stations to the energy situation in Germany.

               To provide information concerning the safety
               of electricity production from nuclear
               energy sources, during a period of considerable
               public concern.

Execution: Campaign was produced rapidly, but within the
               context of an extensive and sophisticated
               on-going program of public information sponsored
               by Germany's electricity producers. Advertising
               agency (Die Werbe/Euro-Advertising, Essen) worked
               with the professional staff of the organization's
               information office in Bonn; all advertising
               was prepared in a conventional client-agency
               relationship, but approved at top management
               level by representatives of the member organizations.

Media: National consumer magazines, magazines with
               consumerist orientation, and spots on the ARD
               and ZDF television stations (German First Program,
               with strong regional orientation and the Second
               Program with only national broadcasting.)

               (A supplementary activity was conducted in
               North Germany by a regional electricity producer
               in an area where agitation against an established
               nuclear power station had emerged. Media used
               were regional newspapers: Die Welt/Hamburg edition,
               Welt am Sonntag/Hamburg edition, Hamburger Abend-
               blatt, and Bild Zeitung/Hamburg edition.)

Results: Strong national public support. Regional
               agitation was reduced when the public in the
               areas concerned was provided with the facts
               concerning the power station which concerned them.

Advertisement reproduction courtesy of Informationszentrale
der Elektrizitaetswirtschaft.

Wie ist das mit dem radioaktiven Abfall?

Die spezielle Eigenart des Abfalls von Kernkraftwerken
(Radioaktivität) erfordert viel Aufwand,
damit keine Schäden für die Umwelt eintreten können.
Es gibt gasförmige, flüssige
und feste radioaktiv verunreinigte Abfälle.

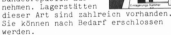

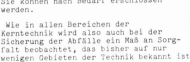

Die gasförmigen radioaktiven Abfälle.
Sie werden so lange innerhalb des Kern-
kraftwerkes zurückgehalten, bis ein
großer Teil der Aktivität abgeklungen
ist. (Radioaktivität zerfällt!) Die
langlebigen radioaktiven Teile gelangen
schließlich über den
Kamin hoch in die Luft.
Doch selbst das bringt
eine Strahlendosis von
weniger als 1 Millirem
pro Jahr für Personen
in der unmittelbaren Um-
gebung eines Kernkraft-
werkes. Dieser Wert ist
110 mal geringer als die
durchschnittliche natür-
liche Strahlenbelastung,
der wir ohnehin ausge-
setzt sind.

Die flüssigen radio-
aktiven Abfälle.
Sie verbleiben in konzentrierter Form in
Filterrückständen, Ionenaustauschern,
als Ergebnis der Abwasseraufbereitung.
Sie werden durch Zumischen von Zement
oder Bitumen verfestigt und kommen in
speziellen Fässern zur Endlagerung.

Die festen radioaktiven Abfälle.
So nennt man Gegenstände, die aktiviert
wurden, oder durch radioaktive Stoffe
verunreinigt sind. Kleidungsstücke zum
Beispiel. Oder Geräte. Auch sie kommen
nach einer Abklingphase
in Sicherheitsbehältern
zur Endlagerung.

... und was geschieht
mit den verbrauchten
Brennelementen? Auch bei
Ihnen wartet man das
Abklingen der kurz-
lebigen Radioaktivität
ab. Anschließend kommen
sie in eine Wiederauf-
bereitungsanlage. Der
hier wiedergewonnene
Brennstoff geht zurück
in den Reaktor. Das
Abfallmaterial wird
nach Verfestigung zu keramischen
Gläsern in die Endlagerung überführt.

Beim Transport radioaktiver Stoffe ...
tauchen besondere Sicherheitsprobleme
auf. Selbst bei schweren Verkehrsun-
fällen darf keine Aktivität entweichen,
um die Bevölkerung nicht zu
gefährden. Ein Behälter
zum Transport von
bestrahlten Brenne-
menten muß zum Beispiel
folgendes aushalten:
Einen freien Fall aus
9 m Höhe. Wobei er mit
seiner empfindlich-
sten Stelle
(Schweißnaht) auf
eine Stahlplatte
trifft, die ein
Betonfundament bedeckt. Ein halbstün-
diges Feuer von über 800 Grad Celsius.
Einen längeren Aufenthalt in 15 Meter
Wassertiefe. Er muß hierbei absolut
dicht und undurchlässig bleiben.

Die Endlagerung.
Die Fachwelt bezeichnet Salzbergwerke
wie die stillgelegte Grube Asse II
bei Wolfsbüttel als "wahrscheinlich
beste Ablageplätze der Welt."
In 490-800 Meter Tiefe
befinden sich die
Lagerkammern. Kein
Wassereinbruch, kein
Erdbeben kann die
Lagersicherheit be-
einträchtigen. Sicher-
heitsmaßnahmen ver-
hindern, daß der Abfall
in unbefugte Hände
kommt. Allein Asse II
könnte bis weit über
das Jahr 2000 hinaus
alle radioaktiven
Abfälle aus der
Bundesrepublik auf-
nehmen. Lagerstätten
dieser Art sind zahlreich vorhanden.
Sie können nach Bedarf erschlossen
werden.

Wie in allen Bereichen der
Kerntechnik wird also auch bei der
Sicherung der Abfälle ein Maß an Sorg-
falt beobachtet, das bisher auf nur
wenigen Gebieten der Technik bekannt ist

Informieren Sie sich. Schreiben Sie uns.

IZE - Informationszentrale der Elektrizitätswirtschaft e.V.,
53 Bonn, Heinrich-Lübke-Straße 19

Die Frage:

"Warum wird
eigentlich
nicht mehr
Ruhrkohle
in Kraftwerken
eingesetzt?"

Karl-Heinz Rehrmann, Bergkamen-Oberaden

Die Antwort:

Welche der Primärenergien Kohle, Öl, Gas oder Uran zur Stromerzeugung in Kraftwerken eingesetzt werden, ist im wesentlichen eine Frage der Kosten und der Sicherheit der Versorgung. Jedes Stromerzeugungsunternehmen muß sich bemühen, die Kilowattstunde kostengünstig herzustellen, um den Strom möglichst preiswert an die Kunden liefern zu können.

Die deutsche Steinkohle ist aus vielerlei Gründen im Vergleich zu den anderen Brennstoffen und zur Importkohle sehr teuer. Damit sie in der Vergangenheit im energiepolitisch gewünschten Umfang überhaupt zur Stromerzeugung eingesetzt werden konnte, mußte der Staat sie subventionieren. Seit dem 1. 1. 1975 werden über den sogenannten Kohlepfennig hierfür einseitig die Stromverbraucher zur Kasse gebeten.

Trotzdem ist der Einsatz deutscher Steinkohle in den Kraftwerken im Jahre 1975 zurückgegangen. Dies hatte mehrere Ursachen. Zum einen nahm der Stromabsatz hauptsächlich aus konjunkturellen Gründen ab, so daß insgesamt weniger Primärenergien benötigt wurden. Zum anderen reichten die erheblichen Subventionen für die Steinkohle nicht aus, um die großen Kostenvorteile der anderen Primärenergien wettzumachen.

Im Interesse der Sicherheit der Energieversorgung sollte die deutsche Steinkohle auch in Zukunft in einem ausgewogenen Verhältnis zur Stromerzeugung eingesetzt werden, um über eine möglichst breite Basis an Primärenergien zu verfügen. Ein der unternehmerischen Eigenverantwortung widersprechender Einsatz über ein technisch und wirtschaftlich vernünftiges Maß hinaus muß die elektrische Energie allerdings unnötig verteuern.
Hierdurch wird nicht nur der stromverbrauchende Haushalt zusätzlich belastet, sondern letztlich auch die Konkurrenzfähigkeit der gesamten deutschen Wirtschaft beeinträchtigt und damit eine Vielzahl von Arbeitsplätzen gefährdet.

Dr. Hans Werner Oberlack
Mitglied des Vorstands der
Hamburgischen Electricitäts-Werke

**Es wird immer genügend Strom geben. Wenn wir vorsorgen.
Mit Kraftwerken, auch Kernkraftwerken, und Leitungen.**

IZE-Informationszentrale der Deutschen Elektrizitätswirtschaft, 5300 Bonn, Heinrich-Lübke-Straße 19

Norway

Kreditkassen
(Christiana Bank og Kreditkasse)

1974-1975

Objective: To clarify misunderstandings about commercial
              banking operations, and to build the people's
              trust in the banking system as such, during a
              period when the Norwegian Government was advoca-
              ting major changes in order to make banking
              "more democratic." (Norwegian Government White
              Paper, No. 99, May 1974.)

Execution: The concept of using an advertising campaign to
              state the facts was initiated by the bank's
              Board of Directors. Planning was carried out
              by a team of marketing and public relations
              experts at the bank's advertising agency, Holter,
              Young & Rubicam A/S, and its public relations
              agency, PPR International, Oslo. In a matter
              of weeks, a general plan and 9 advertisement
              subjects were created and placed. The bank's
              Executive Committee, Board of Directors, and
              public relations department were directly in-
              volved in the development of the advertising
              messages.

Media: Daily newspapers, consumer magazines, brochure
              insert in Reader's Digest (Norway edition),
              and posters for use in bank windows and at
              highway sites.

Results: Campaign impact was studied by means of a public
              opinion survey conducted by Norsk Gallup Institute
              A/S, and evaluated by Holter, Young & Rubicam A/S.
              Attitudes of respondents who reported they had
              seen the campaign were compared with those of
              respondents who had not. A significantly larger
              percentage of those reporting exposure to the
              advertising (1) supported the existing system
              and (2) believed that banks should advertise
              their opinions on public issues.

Advertisement reproduction Courtesy of Christiana Bank og
Kreditkasse, Oslo, Norway.

This is the small and powerful group of owners in Kreditkassen.

cendesse videantur. Invitat igitur neque hominy infant aut iniuste fact si effecerit, et opes vel fortunag vel i volent sib conciliant et, aptissim est peccand quaert en imigent cupidat a

is parend non est nihil enim desid in his rebus emolument oariunt iniur. It sed quiran cunditat vel plurify. Nam luptat plenior efficit. Tia non ob ea so sed mult etiam mag quod cuis. Guae expetend quam nostras expetere quo lo tamet eum locum seque facil, ut mihi de sic amicitiand neg posse a luptate dis

s plena sit, ratiodipsa monet pariender luptam seiung non po amititiao non modo fautrices fi Lorem ipsum dolor si amet, incidunt ut labore et dolore nostrud exercitation ullamc

autem vel eum irur dolore eu fugiat nulla p praesant luptatum provident, simil fuga. Et haru eligend opti assumenda

n nece
rerum hic
cum te

paulo ante cum memorite tum etia ergat. augendas cum conscient to factor tum neque pecum modut est neque nonor im nulla praid om undant. Improb pary m dodecendesse videantur. Invitat igitur v neque hominy infant aut iniuste fact est si effecerit, et opes vel fortunag vel ing volent sib conciliant et, aptissim est ad q peccand quaert en imigent cupidat a nat sunt is parend non est nihil enim desid in his rebus emolument oariunt iniur sed quiran cunditat vel plurify. Nam luptat plenior efficit. Tia non ob ea sol

mult etiam mag quod cuis. Guae nd quam nostras expetere quo loc um locum seque facil, ut mihi det and neg posse a luptate disce it, ratiodipsa monet amicitia m seiung non poest. Atqu o fautrices filelssim i amet, consectetur dolore magna aliq ncorper suscipit dolor in repreh r. At vero ue duos dol culpa qui est er ex t doming

Banking's future is your concern. Take a point of view.

K KREDITKASSEN
- the bank for most people.

Turkey

Elektronik Cihaz Imalatcilari Dernegi
(ECID)

1974-1975

Objective: To encourage the Turkish population to conserve the
                 "hard" currency of the country by purchasing
                 television sets manufactured in Turkey, in preference
                 to those brought into the country by Turkish laborers
                 working in Western European countries.

Execution: Campaign represents a joint effort of all major
                 electronics producers established in Turkey.
                 Individual advertisement subjects were cleared
                 with management representatives of all the companies.

Media: Daily newspapers in large cities.

Results: The campaign is considered "extremely successful."
                 Few Turkish workers today bring foreign-made
                 TV sets with them upon return from work periods
                 outside the country, having learned the advantages
                 of purchasing locally-made ones. ECID consider
                 that the campaign has not only reached but exceeded
                 its target.

Advertisement reproduction Courtesy of Elektronik Cihaz
Imalatcilar Dernegi.

Bir acı yeter

Ölüm bir acıdır.
Çoğu kez çiçek gönderilerek paylaşılan.

Bir acıyı böyle paylaşmak,
bir başka acı doğurmaktır aslında.
Yetenekli ama maddî olanaktan yoksun
nice gencimizin öğrenim umudunu
soldurmak, söndürmektir.

Oysa bu taptaze umutlar,
Türk Eğitim Vakfı'nın
o anlamlı, o ölümsüz çelenkleriyle
yeşerir, yaşar, gerçekleşir.

Çiçek çelenkleriyle
ikinci bir acı yaratmayın.
Kendiniz için de. Toplumumuz için de.

**Yetenekli ama olanaksız
gençlerimizin
öğrenim umudunu
TEV çelenkleriyle yaşatın!**

Türk Eğitim Vakfı

Meclisi Mebusan Cad. 81, Kat 2, Fındıklı — İstanbul
Tel: 45 45 48 - 49 80 10 - 49 80 11
İzmir Tel: 41 751

Turkey

Turk Egitim Vakfi
(TEV)

1973-1975, and continuing

Objective: To encourage the public to take the sums of money
                  traditionally spent on elaborate wreaths and
                  floral displays at funerals, and contribute this
                  money instead to establish scholarships in a
                  national educational fund.

Execution: While the objective of the campaign involved
                  overcoming strongly-entrenched tradition, the
                  planning and execution of the advertising was
                  handled in a conventional relationship between
                  TEV as client and Manajans A.S. as advertising
                  agency.

Media: Daily newspapers in large metropolitan areas.
                  Three waves: autumn 1973, autumn 1974, spring
                  1975. The campaign was renewed in 1976.

Results: The campaign produced a significant level of
                  contributions to the national educational fund
                  and hence was extended initially for two seasons,
                  and now represents a continuing campaign. Results
                  are described by TEV as "heartwarming," with a
                  100% increase of contributions during the
                  latest campaign.

Advertisement reproduction Courtesy of Turk Egitim Vakfi.

174

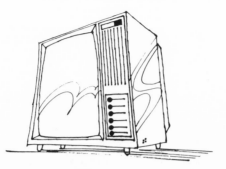

Yerli mi?
Yabancı mı?

Hangisi
ülkemiz şartlarına uygundur?

Bilir misiniz ki...
Yalnız son 12 ayda, işçilerimiz kanalıyla,
yaklaşık 210 milyon TL karşılığı döviz
harcanarak, 60.000 televizyon cihazı
getirilmiştir ülkemize. Ve bunlar,
— televizyon fiyatı 5.000 lira olan bu ülkede
ortalama 7.500 liradan satılmıştır.

Oysa bilirsiniz ki...
Dünyanın en ünlü markaları,
artık yurdumuzda yapılmaktadır.
Türk yapımı televizyonlar, gerek malzeme,
gerekse patent ve teknoloji bakımından
her türlü garantiye sahip, 1. sınıf cihazlardır.

Gene bilirsiniz ki...
Her televizyon, kullanılacağı ülkenin
yayım şartları dikkate alınarak yapılır.
Ve Türkiye'nin yayım şartlarına en uygun
cihazlar, Türk yapımı televizyonlardır.

Ve bilirsiniz ki...
Yabancı yapımı cihazların
Türkiye dışında garanti geçerliği olmasına
karşılık, Türk yapımı cihazlar,
Türkiye'nin her yerinde garanti, servis ve
yedek parça üstünlüğüne sahiptir.

Öyleyse, hangisi ülkemiz şartlarına daha uygun?..
Yerli mi? Yabancı mı?

Bu soruyu, bugüne kadar
1 milyonu aşkın Türk ailesi doğru cevaplandırdı.
Türk yapımı televizyonlar hepsini mutlu etti.

Sizi de mutlu kılacağı gibi.

ECİD
Elektronik Cihaz İmalâtçıları Derneği

India

Government of India
Nirodh (condom) family planning program

1968 to present, continuing

Objective: To gain acceptance for the use of the Nirodh
                 condom as a means to family planning and
                 population control.

                 Substantial resistance in terms of traditional
                 attitudes toward family formation, and toward the
                 physical aspects of sexual relationships, had to
                 be overcome.

Execution: The Government of India worked with six major
                 companies, employing their distribution networks
                 to introduce the Nirodh condom into 170,000
                 retail outlets, and accepting their counsel
                 concerning the development of an advertising
                 campaign.

Media: National newspapers and magazines.

Results: The cost of the condoms and promotion is still
                 subsidized by the Indian Government, but the sales
                 are sufficient for the distributing organizations
                 (Brooke Bond, Hindustan Lever, India Tobacco,
                 Lipton Tea, Tato Oil Mills, and Union Carbide)
                 to recover their costs, while retailers make a
                 small profit. Most recent sales figures for
                 the Nirodh program (1973-1974) indicate an
                 impressive growth in sales. Over 116,000,000
                 pieces were sold, a seven-fold increase over
                 the initial year, 1968.

Information for this case example, and its illustration, have
been obtained from public sources.

Before you have another child
think

wouldn't you first like to give this child all the care she needs?

Life-giving milk. The clothes, the toys, the books...all the things you want to be sure she gets. But if another child should come along too soon, this may not be easy. Wouldn't you prefer to avoid this ?

Millions of couples all over the world are doing just that. They put off having another child till they are ready for it. You too can do so with NIRODH. It's the world's most popular rubber contraceptive for men because it's so safe and simple to use. Why not buy a packet today ?

Available everywhere at only 15 paise for 3 because it is subsidised by the Government.

Until you want another child, use
NIRODH ▼
the safe, simple rubber contraceptive millions choose

Sold by : General Merchants, Chemists and Druggists, Provision Stores, Pan Shops, Etc.

davp 70/580

Sri Lanka

Population Services International

1973 to present, continuing

Objective: To gain acceptance for the use of the
               "Preethi" (joy, happiness) condom as a means
               to family planning and population control.

               Campaign had to overcome ignorance about
               sexual questions, attitudes favoring large
               families, and reluctance to change established
               patterns of behavior.

Execution: The "Preethi" condom was marketed by a private
               non-profit company, rather than by the government.
               Prior to the advertising campaign, Population
               Services International commissioned the research
               division of Lever Brothers, Sri Lanka, to deter-
               mine retailer marketing attitudes, female consumer
               knowledge and practice, and male consumer knowledge
               and practice. Media usership and purchasing behavior
               were also studied. Brand name, package design,
               and advertising messages were pre-tested.

Media: Daily newspapers, radio, cinema, and bus cards.
               (Constraints in radio advertising forbid use
               of the word "condom" and promotion of contraceptive
               brands; the "Preethi" message was carried in
               terms of the "joy" and "happiness" of a well-
               planned family.)

               The campaign was supported by public relations
               activities, including in-store education, dis-
               cussions, leaflets, and sampling.

Results: First-year sales totalled about four million,
               far beyond initial projections. The "Preethi"
               campaign is thought to have involved a larger
               proportion of the population in a shorter time
               than any other family planning program ever
               undertaken.

Advertisement reproduction Courtesy of Population Services
International.

Now!

Preethi
a trusted way to plan your family

simple, safe, sure

▲ Packet of 3
for only 40cts

Look for this
Dispenser
in the shops ▶

preethi
a trusted way to
plan your family
SIMPLE, SAFE,
SURE.

pack of three 40 cts.

"Rely on Preethi...
a trusted way to plan
your family

Preethi is simple,
safe, sure.

"Masagana 99"
Department of Agriculture and Natural Resources
Government of the Philippines

1973-1974

Objective: To convince skeptical farmers to change from
              their traditional methods of raising rice and to
              adopt new agricultural technology, with the aid
              of government loans. ("Masagana 99" is a way
              of expressing in the Tagalog language the target
              of a bountiful harvest of 99 sacks of rice per
              hectare.)

Execution: Following three years of catastrophic rice
              harvests, the Philippine Government assigned the
              task of persuading farmers to use new high-
              yielding rice varieties and the techniques required
              to grow them to the J. Walter Thompson Company
              advertising agency, Manila. JWT participated in
              national planning meetings and handled the develop-
              ment of the advertising by use of a conventional
              agency account team. This was the first time
              the Philippine Government had used an advertising
              agency.

Media: Principally radio: 54 regional early-morning
              daily broadcasts (live, in multiple languages
              depending on area), plus spot reminders and
              jingles in six languages.

              In addition, 4-color supplement in magazines, a
              booklet in 6 languages of explanations and
              instructions (500,000 copies distributed), posters,
              600 bank billboards, stickers, membership flags
              for participating farmers, and informational
              seminars.

Results: Campaign was launched in May, 1973, and was the
              largest radio effort the Philippines has ever
              experienced. By June, 1974, awareness among
              Filipino farmers was high, and 45% of the rice
              farmer population were participating in the rice
              production program. Most important, harvest of
              rice rose by 26.1% over the previous 12 months.
              The agency's achievement was publicly commended
              by President Marcos, who gave JWT the "Presidential
              Golden Plow Award For Public Service."

NOTE: This case does not strictly qualify for inclusion as an
example, because the agency donated staff time and overhead costs,
and the radio stations donated air time. However, in all other
ways the campaign was handled as a conventional advertising/public
relations effort.

Illustrative materials reproduction Courtesy of Government of
the Philippines and J. Walter Thompson Company.

ANG **BINAG-O** NGA **PAAGI** SANG **MASAGANA 99**

181

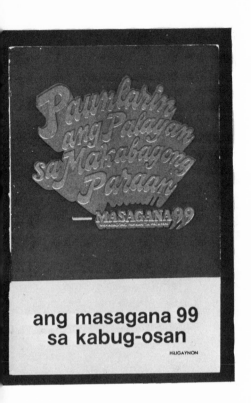

ang masagana 99
sa kabug-osan

HILIGAYNON

general information
on masagana 99

ENGLISH

183

Multi-National (base country, Netherlands)

Philips Industries
1974, continuing

Objective :   To inform the target audiences about Philips
capabilities which contribute to the solution
of problems that are important   to society
at-large or groups in it.

The more technical and professionally oriented
part of the campaign has a more specific sub-
-objective : To inform the various industrial
and professional target groups about what
Philips offers to prospective customers.

Execution :   Two basic campaigns, "institutional" (aimed at
international decision makers) and "professional
(pre-determined target groups amongst public
authorities, industry, government and the
professions) were created by two advertising
agencies working in cooperation with a campaign
team of the advertising department at concern
headquarters in Eindhoven, Netherlands. Subjects
are proposed and approved by members of combined
agency/company team in which top international
advertising management level is represented.

Media :   "Institutional" campaign : 4-colour full-pages
in international general-interest magazines
(Time International, Newsweek International,
National Geographic, Vision Lat. America.)

"Professional" campaign : black-and-white double-
-page spreads in magazines segmented according
to special interest (Business Week, The Economist,
International Herald Tribune, etc.), according
to profession (architects, engineers, scientists,
etc.) and according to region (Far Eastern
Economic Review, Middle East Trade, Africa, etc.)

In addition to advertising, Philips publishes
a magazine, Philips Professional Profile, which
describes problems of general interest and
Philips' work in helping to solve them.

Results :   "Professional" advertisements, carrying a keyed
coupon offering additional information, have
produced thousands of inquiries of high quality.
In addition, Philips has received many letters
and telephone calls from all over the world.

Advertisement reproduction Courtesy of Philips Industries.

Solar Energy is at home here.

This house in Aachen, West Germany, may hold the key to our future energy needs. Built jointly by Philips, RWE Essen and the Federal Government, it utilises solar energy and the natural energy stored in the ground for heating and cooling purposes. The energy consumption of the house has been minimised by the use of improved insulation and a new double glazing system. It's still at the experimental stage, but it could take us towards a more efficient use of the huge supply of free energy which Nature offers us.

A 20 m² area of the roof holds 324 Philips solar collectors which convert solar energy into heat of up to 95°C - even when the sun doesn't shine. On average about 10,000 to 12,000 kWh of energy is collected per year - more than enough to cover the entire heating needs of the house.
Supervising the experiment is a Philips mini-computer which simulates the behaviour of an average family of four, while another computer processes the data and controls the heating.

PHILIPS   Working on energy conservation.

<u>Multi-National (Base Area -- Europe)</u>

ITT Europe, Inc.

1974 to present, continuing

<u>Objective</u>:   In the face of strong criticism of ITT inter-
nationally as a multinational corporation, to
position the many separate units of ITT Europe
as contributors to the national economies of
the countries in which they operate.

To explain the relationship between the individual
units and ITT, and show how being part of ITT
enhances their effectiveness and contribution.

<u>Execution</u>:   ITT Europe undertook a long series of image/attitude
research projects in a number of European
countries, beginning in 1969, using the Landell
Mills research organization. The United Kingdom
was designated as the first country in which a
corporate advertising approach was to be tested.
Development of a campaign was assigned to KMP,
London advertising agency associated with ITT's
international corporate agency, Needham, Harper
& Steers. Seven separate campaign approaches
were developed (including a cartoon approach)
and pre-tested before the final campaign was agreed
upon. All developmental work was supervised by
the ITT Europe public relations group in Brussels.
In addition to the careful pre-testing (which
indicated a need to strike a balance between
factual information, attention-getting elements,
and emotional tone), all advertisements were
subject to approval by multiple management levels
within ITT. First wave of the U.K. campaign was
released in fall, 1974, and continued in 1975.
A follow-up campaign with identical objectives and
a similar creative approach was launched in October,
1976, and will run through May, 1977.

On the basis of research and the U.K. experience,
a basic strategy was spelled out. Individual
campaigns would be planned for each European
country, concentrating on the subjects of national
concern indicated by the continuing image/attitude
research studies. Preparation and testing of
campaigns were undertaken by the Needham, Harper
& Steers affiliates in France and Spain, and
further launches are planned for 1977 and beyond.

<u>Media</u>:   U.K. advertising was directed to a "high-level
target audience," using national newspapers with
a strong business orientation (<u>The Times</u>, <u>Financial</u>

"Why would ITT want to invest in Britain at a time like this?"

For many years now, ITT companies have been investing in the British economy in a big way.

Since early 1970, for example, their investment in buildings, equipment and machinery in the UK has totalled £43 million, much of it in Government designated development areas.

Not to mention the £76 million that went into British research, development and engineering during the same period.

All of which is long term investment, with export and employment implications stretching into the 80s and beyond.

But what about 1975 itself?

And what about all those gloomy forecasts about Britain's future?

As far as ITT is concerned, there were good reasons for investing in Britain for the last 50 years. And there are equally good reasons this year.

So ITT companies plan to invest at least another £12 million on buildings, equipment and machinery in Britain during 1975.

Which represents not only a £4 million increase on the ITT average over the last five years, but also a pretty unambiguous vote of confidence in Britain's long term future.

Times, Guardian, Telegraph, The Observer) and serious opinion reviews (New Statesman, The Economist, New Scientist, Spectator). The same strategy was to be extended to the other national markets in which the campaign approach would be introduced.

Results:

Initial spontaneous reactions in the U.K; were strongly favorable. Subsequent voluntary reactions (stimulated by a coupon invitation in a full-page newspaper advertisement reproducing the initial advertising subjects) attracted more than 5,000 letters and requests for further information on ITT. Notwithstanding the general level of criticism of multinational corporations, the 5,000 letters included no more than 20 with negative comments of any kind, and ITT regard this as a major accomplishment.

Continuing image/attitude research (conducted by Landell Mills Associates) confirmed a favorable shift of British opinion concerning ITT in the U.K. The survey (in-depth interviews with top business, government, and professional figures) was carried out in 12 European countries in addition to the U.K., reaching more than 5,800 individuals and provided a means of comparing the attitudes generated by the ITT U.K. campaign with current attitudes toward ITT, IBM, and ICI (other sponsors of the research) in the 13 countries covered.

On the basis of the research findings, activity to extend the ITT approach generated in the U.K. continues, with the individual countries preparing' their own campaigns. The basic strategy has been set, and liaison and approval channels with ITT Europe and ITT's New York headquarters established.

Advertisements reproduction Courtesy of ITT Europe, Inc.

"Why should ITT care tuppence about British technology?"

With its Headquarters in the United States, ITT might be expected to concentrate its research effort there, too.

But it doesn't.

On the contrary, wherever ITT does business, it also invests in research and development.

In Britain, for example, ITT employs over 2,000 scientists and engineers on research and development, a quarter of them at Standard Telecommunication Laboratories, Harlow, the largest of ITT's four major research centres in Europe.

Among the research fields pioneered at Harlow has been that of fibre optics, which has the potential to transmit hundreds of thousands of separate telephone conversations over a glass thread no thicker than a human hair.

Apart from playing its part in helping to maintain Britain's status as a technological world leader, ITT's research investment policy has made an impact in terms of hard cash.

Over the last five years, ITT has invested over £38 million in British research, £11.5 million in 1974 alone. And if associated engineering costs are included, the five year total comes up to over £76 million.

Which is a good deal more than tuppence in anybody's language.

For further information, including a new 20-page publication "Facts about ITT in Europe", please write to 190 Strand, London WC2R 1DU.
ITT companies in Britain include:
Abbey Life Assurance, Ashe Laboratories, Excess Insurance,
ITT Consumer Products, Rimmel, Sheraton,
Standard Telephones and Cables and Standard Telecommunication Laboratories.